Breakfast at the Hoito

Breakfast at the
HOITO
and Other Adventures
in the Boreal Heartland

Charles Wilkins

Natural Heritage Books

Breakfast at the Hoito
and Other Adventures in the Boreal Heartland
Charles Wilkins

Natural Heritage / Natural History Inc.

Published by Natural Heritage / Natural History Inc.
(P.O. Box 95, Station O, Toronto, Ontario, M4A 2M8)

Design by Steve Eby
Printed and bound in Canada by Hignell Printing Limited, Winnipeg, Manitoba.

Second Printing

Canadian Cataloguing in Publication Data
Wilkins, Charles
    Breakfast at the Hoito : and other adventures in the boreal heartland
Includes Index.
ISBN 1-896219-33-0

1. Superior, Lake, Region.   2. Ontario, Northern.
I. Title.
FC3095.S86W54 1997 971.3'12 C97-931688-X
F1059.S9W54 1997

THE CANADA COUNCIL   LE CONSEIL DES ARTS
FOR THE ARTS   DU CANADA
SINCE 1957   DEPUIS 1957

Natural Heritage / Natural History Inc. acknowledges the support received for its publishing program from the Canada Council Block Grant Program. We also acknowledge with gratitude the assistance of the Association for the Export of Canadian Books, Ottawa.

for my daughters Georgia and Eden
Thunder Babies

Table of Contents

Introduction

FOR THE PAST SEVEN YEARS, northwestern Ontario has been the stimulus and setting for much of my writing, including twenty or more magazine articles. The latter are a testament to what I know and like best about this part of the country: the forests, the lakes, the old mountains, the wildlife, Lake Superior... and of course the people, most of whom have, in one way or another, been dreamed and dealt, and sometimes damned, by the landscape they inhabit.

I am happy to include in this collection stories on a variety of individuals and groups, and in particular on the Finns, Italians and local Anishnabe, each of whom I admire for their strength and their enduring cultures.

I am also pleased to include several brief personal pieces, not so much as a record of a specific time or place but of the longer arc of a life.

The stories are arranged not chronologically but in the order that seemed to suit the subjects and flow. All but two of them — "Breakfast at the Hoito" and "Thunder Bay: More Personal and Better Imagined" — have been published in Canadian magazines.

Because several of the stories were originally written as far back as five years ago, I have attempted to put each into context with a new and separate introduction... and thereby feel justified in keeping my *introductory* introduction to a minimum.

As alway, I wish to thank my wife, Betty, and my children, Matthew, Georgia and Eden for their forebearance and love, and for their tolerance of the writing-caused chaos that so often seems to swallow up our lives. I owe them a lot.

My thanks, too, to my editor Jane Gibson and publisher Barry Penhale at Natural Heritage — for suggesting the book in the first place and for accommodating the unorthodoxies of my work habits. And to Ann Vanderhoof and Ian Darragh, who commissioned and published a number of these stories while they were editors, respectively, of *Cottage Life* and *Canadian Geographic* magazines.

Finally, a special thanks to Ann and Nelson King, Alf Petrone, Kal Nikkila, Kathleen McFadden and Pat Forrest, without whose timely and generous support there would be no book.

Breakfast at the Hoito

Like any local hero or old friend, the Hoito restaurant needs no introduction to regional readers and diners. It is one of the most historic restaurants in Canada and, in its characteristic way, one of the best and best-known. I have nothing more to say by way of introduction, either to the place or to the story that follows, than to express a regret that I have not mentioned by name every Hoito employee who was kind enough to chat with me and broaden my experience of the restaurant during two hot days spent in the kitchen last June. My thanks, respect and good wishes to all of them.

HOITO RESTAURANT IN THUNDER BAY—"the Hoito" as everybody calls it—occupies the basement of the Finn Hall, a commodious old brick pile in the city's original Finnish quarter on Bay Street. Unlike more recent Finnish buildings, with their sinuous lines and Arctic contours, the hall would seem to have been designed by a dreamy cabal of 19th-century tinker-toy builders. Almost every one of its features—from the porch columns and side-turrets to the central tower with its silvered dunce-cap and Eastern cupola—suggests an afterthought to the H-shaped box at the centre of it all. Aesthetically, the most flattering perspective on the place is from the lookout in Hillcrest Park where, give or take an angle or two, its vast grey roof shows the satisfying dimensions of an elephant's back.

But nobody is burdened by such thoughts as they descend the stairs into the restaurant, which serves between 500 and 800 meals a day, and can stretch the hungriest customer to the limit with its strenuous Finnish cuisine. The menu is a throwback to the days when immigrant Finnish loggers roamed Bay Street, and the routine breakfast of such men consisted of a bowl of oatmeal porridge, half a dozen pancakes, an equal number of sausages, a plate-sized omelette and a six-inch stack of thickly-buttered rye

The Finn Hall and Hoito during the 1950s.

bread—all washed down with three or four cups of prescription-strength coffee. Dinner was soup, salad, a bowl of *mojakka* (a beef stew heavy on root vegetables), a pound of roast pork or fillet of lake trout, three or four boiled potatoes, gravy, corn, peas, another six-inch stack of rye bread and half an apple pie. Depending on circumstances and tastes, a Finnish meal might also have included a slice or two of traditional salt fish or *suolakala*, made from imported salmon or locally caught trout, a slab or two of cardamom-flavoured coffee bread and a bear's helping of rice pudding or *viili*, a yogurt-like dish described as "clabbered milk" on the current Hoito menu and customarily served with homemade strawberry or blueberry sauce. Meals of such exaggerated variety and profusion wouldn't typically have been available in restaurants of the day, except that, from its beginnings in 1918 until the early 1960s, the Hoito mimicked the bush camps by serving its food on large platters at communal tables—all you could eat for 25 cents during the '30s, a dollar during the '60s. The original character of the Hoito was so similar to that of the logging kitchens that, for decades, the restaurant would not hire a cook who did not have bush camp experience.

Today, nobody could eat such meals without killing themselves. But the Hoito offers edited versions of them so compelling and reasonably priced that, almost every week-day at noon and supper hour, a line-up of customers is willing to wait up to fifteen minutes for a table in the 110-seat restaurant. By late morning on an average Sunday—brunch day in Thunder Bay—there are a dozen or more customers waiting in the entranceway for seats. As they get them, new people take their places, with the result that the evolving gaggle of pancake-lovers around the door—students, young families, Finnish pensioners—sometimes persists for two hours or more while the kitchen pulses and the cash register clangs. Those who want to avoid line-ups go at (slightly) off hours…or go by themselves, knowing that, whatever the time of day, there is invariably an empty stool at the 16-seat counter.

The first meal I ate in Thunder Bay was at the Hoito. I'd flown in from Toronto on a hot day in July, 1991, to begin a two-week teaching stint at the Curtis School of the Arts at Confederation College. The young woman who coordinated the school met me at the airport and, having determined that I hadn't eaten on my flight, ferried me immediately to "this really great Finnish place," where I scarfed up a Sunday special that included cream of chicken soup, Kivela rye bread, coleslaw, peas, a heap of mashed potatoes and a bumper ham steak about as big around as a French beret. For dessert, I had pumpkin pie with whipped cream and as much good coffee as I could drink. Needless to say, I didn't have a clue about the Hoito's roots, or its significance in the community, but I was well impressed by its unpretentiousness and by the casual good will obvious among the customers and between the customers and waitresses. The meal, *tout complet*, cost me $6.50, a value which so inspired me that I showed up the following night for a $7.25 meal of pea soup, pork chops, and lemon pie.

I moved to Thunder Bay with my family in the autumn of that year, and since then have eaten perhaps 300 meals at the Hoito. My daughters, Georgia and Eden, aged 3 and 2, were Hoito veterans long before they took a bite of solid food. Matthew, aged 9, has eaten his weight in Finnish pancakes. I have sent people there, and taken people there, among them every ill-nourished writer who has ever paid a call on me in the city. When Gordie Howe, a friend from my sportswriting days, visited Thunder Bay in 1992, my wife Betty and I, hoping to provide him with a genuine core sample of the city, took him, first, up to Hillcrest Park to see the lake and elevators, then down to Bay Street for breakfast at the Hoito.

Much to its credit, the Hoito is not to everyone's tastes. Yet it is certainly one of the more distinctive expressions of the fabric of the city and area. It is one of the few such expressions that can be experienced indoors (others I can think of are the Kangas Sauna, the Scandinavian Home, and the Italian and Da Vinci halls). The Hoito's appeal is so obvious that I have at times speculated on why there aren't more places like it, and why they never seem to exist in other cities. If a reason can be articulated, it would appear to lie not in desirability but in the simple truth that "to everything there is a season," and that the season for starting such places and developing their foundations has passed and is not coming back. A restaurant *like* the Hoito would have to have been built, as the Hoito was, at a time, and under conditions, and on principles—and, most significantly, amidst people and a culture—that inspired in its founders a genuine concern for the common person. Rare in the past, unheard of today. Good luck to the philanthropic restaurateur in an era when profit rules the market, "growth" is a mantra, and the world's most successful diner thrives under the rubric "billions and billions served."

But with deep roots in the community and a vaulting head start, the Hoito continues doing more or less what it set out to do when, at the end of World War I, a group of local Finns decided that immigrant Finnish bush workers needed a place in Port Arthur to get a hearty meal at an affordable price. The idea is said to have germinated at Kallio's bush camp near Nipigon and have travelled to the city, where dozens of prospective customers kicked in a few dollars each. When the pot reached $300, the organizers hired a cook and some waitresses, and the Hoito was born. From the beginning, the place was run on democratic principles—some might say socialistic. Oldtimers report that no one was ever denied a meal for lack of money, and if business was good, prices went down. Even today, Hoito's owners, the Finnish Building Company, use the restaurant's proceeds not for private gain but to foster local Finnish culture and education. And the employees, as always, receive decent remuneration for their efforts. Today's wages range from $8.15 an hour for beginning kitchen helpers to $12-plus for grill cooks.

Much of which was on my mind when, on a day last June, I walked into the office of the manager, Anneli Smith, and asked if I could spend a couple of shifts in the restaurant's kitchen and recesses, so that I could see exactly how the old institution functioned. My purpose, I explained, was to write about what I saw and heard, and to expose the Hoito if not exactly to the world, at least to a few thousand readers (and to listeners of CBC radio's "Voyage North" for whom I did a two-part, half-hour report).

It is a measure of the integrity and self-confidence of the organization that Anneli granted my request without hesitation, suggesting that we go immediately to the kitchen so that she could introduce me to the head cook, Tuula Granholm, as well as to Sirkka Ahola, one of a handful of employees whose responsibilities include opening the place, alone, two or three mornings a week at 4 a.m.

Sirkka and I agree to meet in the parking lot the following day at 3:45 a.m.—an hour, it turns out, at which the sky is showing the faintest wash of gray light, and the blackbirds have just begun to stir in the ash trees behind the restaurant. I arrive chatty with anticipation, but as we round the building onto Bay Street Sirkka turns to me with her finger at her lips, urging me to shush up, and we tiptoe along the sidewalk in a burlesque of the Beagle Boys approaching the vault. It is not until we are almost at the front doors that I understand her concern. There, in the concrete-enclosed garden, just a few feet away, three men lie sleeping in the shadows. Sirkka's attitude toward them has nothing to do

Sirkka Ahola came to Canada from northern Finland in 1969.

with courtesy—she is afraid to waken them, for fear they might hassle her or attempt to get into the restaurant.

She secures the door quickly and proceeds to the kitchen, where, before punching her time card or even removing her jacket, she grinds a pot's worth of coffee beans, dumps them into a filter, and turns on the coffee maker, so that the day can begin in earnest. Coffee is the Finnish national elixir, and this inaugural pot, made at predawn strength, is the first of 175 (one every four minutes) that the restaurant will brew that day. By mid-morning, the fragrance of the ground beans will be irresistibly hybridized by the smell of fresh strawberry and blueberry sauce bubbling in 5-gallon pots on the nearby stove.

Sirkka emerges from the dressing room and, in apron and hair net, ignites the 20-odd gas jets that heat the ovens and grills along the kitchen's west wall. She then opens a walk-in refrigerator and, on a trolley, extracts a 20-pound saw-log of beef, two 10-pound pork roasts, 12 pounds of bacon, 200 sausages, 200 eggs, 20 pounds of beef parts for the *mojakka*, 15 pounds of precut home fries, two 20-pound tubs of peeled onions and carrots, and enough butter for half a dozen heart attacks... all of it the merest beginnings of the food that will be cooked and consumed over the next sixteen hours.

With her supplies at hand, she runs a 10-gallon pot of water, heaves it onto the stove, and dumps in the beef for the *mojakka*. She runs another such pot and sets it to boil for oatmeal porridge. On a back burner, over low heat, she places a 5-gallon pan of dense brown gravy.

Then the beef and pork roasts go in (when they come out, two immense turkeys will take their place). Sirkka stops at a table on which 28 loaves of bread are stacked, withdraws a couple of slices and throws them onto the conveyer belt of the toaster. By the time they reappear, the coffee is ready, and so are we. As we sit at the staff table, she talks wistfully about growing up in northern Finland, near Oulu—of the fabled winters and midnight sun—and of leaving to come to Canada in 1969. She is in her early 60s, and has worked at the Hoito for seventeen years. Two of her daughters have also worked at the restaurant, and her granddaughter, Melanie Bingham, is now a waitress. Sirkka expresses a hope that Melanie's two-year-old daughter, Sasha—Sirkka's great-granddaughter—will never hold a job in the famous scullery. "I love the place," she says. "It's my second home. But the work is hard—especially in summer, it's so hot." Sirkka is a disciplined, unassuming woman, with a compact physique and an almost beatific smile and personality. She is as durable as snare wire. As I follow her around, I ask repeatedly if I can help her heft this pot of water, this tub of meat, this box of vegetables—in some cases, 40-pound loads—but she won't even acknowledge my offers.

At 4:35, she hauls four plastic pails from the refrigerator, each containing two or three gallons of milk, eggs and oil, mixed the previous night for the hundreds of Finnish pancakes that will be served before the grill is turned off at 7:30 this evening. She adds flour to each pail, not by weight or volume but by an educated "feel" for what the consistency of the batter should be. Pancakes have a grill of their own at the Hoito, and, at almost any time of day, Sirkka or someone else is at that grill minding six or eight pancakes in the process of being cooked. Beside the grill, three 100-ounce cans hold a molten mixture of butter and lard that, before each batch is poured, is swabbed onto the cooking surface with a teensy cotton mop.

Just after 5:00 a.m., the first two waitresses appear (two more will arrive for the breakfast rush a couple of hours hence, and another two by lunchtime). Marketta Valiharju and Paula Malone both began work at the restaurant intending to stay a year or so but have now logged the better part of a decade. "I just wanted to pay off the mortgage," smiles Paula, "but my husband works at the grain elevators, and when they started going down, I stayed put."

The two go briskly to work, grinding coffee, wiping chairs, setting tables, filling syrup and ketchup containers, erasing yesterday's menu board and marking up today's dinner and lunch selections. As they go about their business, Sirkka puts 200 sausages in the oven to roast, pulls six pounds of bacon off the grill and replaces it with fifteen pounds of home fries, to which she adds salt, onion powder and a pound or so of butter. On another part of the grill, she piles 10 pounds of sliced onion that later in the day will be served with Salisbury steak or a long-time Hoito favourite, fried liver.

❖

The restaurant opens at 6:00 a.m., but anywhere up to fifteen minutes prior to that, a corps of aging Finlanders, all of them men, gathers outside in anticipation of the doors being unlocked and of their first bump of caffeine. Arja Maki, one of two or three waitresses who specialize in counter service, and who calls them "my boys," serves their coffee, kibitzes with them in Finnish, and smiles at their jokes. "They're great," she says. "I talk to them about everything—their pasts, current affairs, their love lives."

On my second morning in the restaurant, I join the oldtimers at about 6:10 at the counter and am greeted with monumental indifference.

"I'm writing a story about the restaurant," I pipe up eventually. "I'm wondering if I could talk to you fellas about it."

"I don't want my name in no book," one of them says into his coffee.

"Don't put my name in," says another.

"What is your name?" I ask, to which they look at me as if I were senile, or an insect of some sort.

"Them forest fires are gonna take the whole damn country," says a man in a Husqvarna chainsaw hat. "Billions'a dollars gettin burnt up. Ya watchin' the hockey? Ya think it's ever gonna end?"

"I'd like to," says the man seated next to him. "But it's too loud."

"Why don't you turn it down?"

"I can't hear it if I turn it down."

Husqvarna tells an off-colour joke, and his neighbour, after a long sip of coffee, says, "I been watering my tomato plants just about every morning—never used to hafta water them. The rain came in nice. Nuthin ever dried out."

"When was that?"

"Oh, a long time ago."

By 6:30, the first wave of them is gone, and a trickle of breakfast customers has begun to arrive. By this time, the unacknowledged heroes of the restaurant business, the kitchen helpers, are hard at work in the trenches behind the lines. They are the first to make contact with much of the food that makes its way inexorably from the pantries and refrigerators to the ovens, plates, and finally to the customers' stomachs and out the door. There are anywhere up to half a dozen of them in the restaurant at once, and when they are not busy with their knives, graters and peelers, they mop floors, scrub appliances and wash dishes. On this particular morning, Pia Erkkila, a serene young woman who has worked at the Hoito for eight years, is at a prep table dicing onions, tomatoes and ham. During the next couple of hours, she will slice turkey for clubhouse and hot turkey sandwiches; separate the bone, fat and gristle from the *mojakka* beef, which, at this point, is still boiling; bread the liver; shape the burger patties; and, as she puts it, help "plate up" food at the steam table.

A few feet away, Kaisu Kittila, who began the morning by slicing fourteen oranges to be used throughout the day as garnishes, is grating six or seven heads of cabbage for coleslaw. That done, she will begin converting fifteen pounds of lettuce, eight or nine cucumbers and three dozen tomatoes into tossed salad.

The kitchen at the Hoito is just one of a labyrinth of antique rooms that serve the restaurant and its staff in ways unimaginable to the average customer. The staff smoking room, for instance, is a ventilated cubby, about four feet by eight feet, with a concrete floor and two wooden benches, like those in an old-style rink shack. Two small mirrors hang on its walls, and assorted shoes inhabit its corners. On my first morning in the restaurant, a pair of well-thumbed gardening magazines sat atop the benches among hair nets, rubber gloves and several 48-ounce cans, stripped of their labels and partially filled with stubbed cigarettes. The waitresses get no official breaks, but are permitted a meal or a hit of coffee or nicotine at any time they have an opportunity to grab one. Every twenty minutes or so during my first day in the restaurant, one young waitress flew into the smoking room, lit a cigarette and took two furious drags, one on top of the other. Taking momentary care to sequester the butt for future reference, she beat it out the door, exhaling a cubic metre of smoke, and was back among her tables, all within ten or twelve seconds.

The nearby change room, with its low ceiling and windowless beige panelling, is notable only because its lack of charm exceeds even that of the smoking room. The pantries on the other hand are a world of intrigue, containing longstanding Hoito secrets—in cans, in buckets, in bottles…in plastic and paper bags.

Beside those pantries, along the east wall of the building, by the rear door, is the most memorable room of all, an unadorned dungeon housing electrical fixtures, furnace, ice maker and air conditioning equipment…and, in a back corner, camouflaged against the surroundings, a metre-high stack of potatoes in thick burlap sacks. This antediluvian cell, with its concrete floor, moulting brick walls, and naked light bulbs, cannot have been altered significantly since the building opened in 1910. One of its few post-war features is an army-capacity stainless-steel Hobart potato peeler that, every morning at about 5:30, is put rumbling to work removing the skins from 125 pounds of potatoes. Since the machine grinds the skin off, instead of cutting it, its effluent is not so much "peelings" as a gritty, brown paste that, for obvious reasons, gets lighter the longer the machine runs.

On this day, the peeling and potato prep have fallen to a pair of veteran kitchen workers, Mirja Kuoppa-Aho and Eevi Savioja, who, having emptied the now-skinless Idahos into buckets of cold water, sit on upturned five-gallon pails (the preferred stools of the kitchen) chatting exuberantly in Finnish as they carve the eyes from the spuds and cut dozens of them into pieces for *mojakka*. When the work is done, Eevi, a lean-shouldered stoic who emigrated to Canada in 1956, will spend the rest of the shift on dishes. Mirja, who worked eighteen years at the Kestitupa restaurant across the street before coming to the Hoito six years ago, will go to the grill to make pancakes and do short order frying.

The spoken word is far and away the mainstay of communication at the Hoito, but throughout the kitchen and catacombs there is an additional disclosure of values in the form of numerous hand-written signs."TO ORDER OMELETES," says one of them, "PLEASE ORDER HAM, CHEESE, MUSHROOM, INSTEAD OF ANY OTHER ORDER…CHEESE, MUSHROOM, NOT MUSHROOM, CHEESE…HAM, CHEESE, NOT CHEESE, HAM…AND WESTERN, NOT EASTERN."

"WAITRESSES & STAFF," declares another, "ONLY USE STEAK KNIVES ON PIES. CUT INTO 8 PIECES. NO SMALL OR BIG PIECES." The most graphic kitchen directive is a hand-drawn

Last plate of the day: from left: Helvi Roblee, Jenni Glad, Artith Francis, Tiina Heimonen, Pia Heikkinen, Pirkko Sorri (partly hidden), Paula Malone, Elisa Kittila, Kaija Pinta, Angie Makinen and Sinnika Kyrola.

plate on which 13 amorphous shapes indicate the exact position-ing of each item on the Hoito cold plate: pineapple, sliced turkey, salt fish, potato, coleslaw, bean or carrot salad, two and a half dev-illed eggs, lettuce, jelly, sliced onion, sliced cheese, sliced ham and sliced Finnish sausage or *makkara*.

A staff bulletin board bears messages such as: "Call me to come in anytime if I'm not already working—Robyn." And: "Hey, Girls! Go check out the plans for our new area on the board by the dress-ing room." And: "If your hair is fairly long, please keep it in a pony-tail or at least make an effort to keep it neat." At the centre of the board, a ballpoint cartoon depicts a world-weary grill cook looking out from under the banner: IT'S THE ALL-NEW HIT SHOW, COOKIN' WITH THE HOITO! "Okay," the cook is explaining to her audience,"*here we have our can of melted lard on our smokin' hot grill…slather some on and we're ready to cook.*"

Above the west back door of the kitchen are the words: "*Jatan kaiki murheeni tyopaikalleni minulla on nita aivan tarpeeksi kotonakin.*" I leave my worries at the work place. I have enough of them at home.

❖

At 8:30 or 9, the manager Anneli Smith comes in, stylish and proprietary, clearly in charge of her jurisdiction. She opens her office opposite the cashier's booth, heads for the kitchen and downs her habitual breakfast of toast, cheese, tomato, and a single piece of bacon. Anneli was born in Sievi, in central Finland, came to Canada in 1957, and a decade later began a nineteen-year stint as a food services employee at Lakehead University. She had never set foot in the Hoito when, in 1986, she responded to the restaurant's ad for a manager and got the job. By anybody's definition, she is a good boss—open, judicious and good-natured. It is a matter of honour with her that she knows all 57 of her employees by name and that the Hoito enjoys extremely low turnover in staff, despite the intense stresses of restaurant work.

Having finished her breakfast, Anneli chats briefly with the kitchen help, returns to her office and confronts the proliferating jumble of chores—scheduling, invoices, staff needs, holidays, supplies, pricing, customer concerns, equipment, and so on—that will keep her at her desk for the better part of the next nine hours. "There's so much to think about," she says, "that when I wake up in the middle of the night, my mind comes here."

Anneli's closest underling is head cook Tuula Granholm who, at 31, has already posted 18 years at the restaurant and has done every job in the establishment except waitressing, for which she claims to be too shy. She has a homey smile, bright blonde hair and the wide eyes of a water nymph. Her diffident personality belies the prodigious work habits and sense of responsibility without which she would not have lasted an hour, let alone seven years, as head cook. Among other daily chores, she cuts all the restaurant's meat, poultry and fish; prepares and cooks every main dish on the menu; roasts and carves two turkeys; makes all soups; boils and mashes the potatoes and makes the gravy; and makes all pies, desserts and fruit sauces. On Mondays, she makes salt fish; on Tuesdays *piirakat* (a kind of Finnish pita); on Wednesdays *ropsu* (oven pancakes); and on Thursdays cabbage rolls—"rice moccasins," she calls them. When she is not making meals, she receives groceries from suppliers, rotates inventory to avoid spoilage, and makes sure the ingredients are on hand for the next day's menu . Twice a week, she has the onerous responsibility of cleaning the ovens.

At the point I caught up with Tuula on my first morning in the restaurant, she had in front of her a substantial pile of ground beef which she was painstakingly rolling into perfect little balls for the spaghetti sauce. Twenty minutes later, she was applying spices and marinade to several large fillets of salmon that would eventually cross the counter as *suolakala*... and, shortly after that, tending a 5-gallon vessel of fresh strawberry sauce.

At mid-morning, she drained a 10-gallon pot of boiled potatoes, added a gallon or so of milk, a couple of pounds of butter, and set the pot on the floor. She fetched a large two-handled drill-like contraption, placed a foot on either side of the pot, and, wielding the implement like a jackhammer, pushed its three-foot shaft and (as-yet unfunctioning) blade into the potatoes. She turned the machine on, and stood there grimacing as it bucked and heaved, quickly transforming the potatoes into an off-white homogenized mass.

When I asked about the recipe for Finnish rice pudding, my favourite Hoito dessert, Tuula surprised me by saying that she couldn't give me that or any other Hoito recipe—at least in grams, ounces or cups—because none of it had ever been written down, or even thought out in those terms; she makes everything out of her head. "I think people appreciate that the cooking here isn't fully standardized," she said. "I try to keep to the way I was taught, but I improve things too. It's never quite always the same."

Tuula is ultimately accountable for every plate of food that leaves the kitchen, but consumes very little restaurant food herself. "I see so much of it in a day," she says, "that I usually don't feel like eating it." The pressure of the job, she allows, cuts further into her appetite. "I have to be so watchful not to get things burned or overcooked, or dried out after they're cooked. Sometimes I'm doing four or five things at once."

Tension is compounded for Tuula and the staff by the radical confinements of the eighty-year-old kitchen. "It's pretty close quarters," says waitress Rita Rintakangas. "Everybody's always like 's'cuse me', 's'cuse me', 's'cuse me.'... Don't get me wrong; it's the greatest place in the world to work. We're very close—like family." Suddenly Rita is smiling. "What's more stressful than family? Anyway, s'cuse me," she says. "I gotta go." And she is up from the staff table, and out into the dining room, order pad in hand.

Waitresses are the front-line forces, the shock troops and commandos, of any sizeable restaurant operation. The stress of dealing with the customers, of *accommodating* them and *gratifying* them, of doing it quickly and obligingly and politely when issues as pressing as their hunger and money are on the line... of being an agent of their hopes and a sponge for their irritability... doing it for this table of six, this brooding couple, this bunch of teenagers, these frantic parents with their squabbling preschoolers... doing it for friends and relatives and foes, again and again, with a four-star headache, and the kitchen in an uproar, and "I'm sure you said pork chops, Sir."... the stress of it trumps all other restaurant jobs, including standing by a hot grill, pouring pancakes, being splashed by the deep fryer, dealing with ten plateloads at a time, or simultaneously cooking turkeys and casseroles and potatoes. "There's just nothing compares to it," says one Hoito employee who has been both a kitchen helper and a waitress—which is why many kitchen workers will happily sacrifice thousands of dollars in annual tips, and are generally willing to stay forever backstage, unrecognized and unheralded, so long as they don't have to do even three or four times in a career what any competent waitress has to do fifty times a day to keep her job.

For the waitresses and kitchen staff, the Hoito's weekday breakfast rush is little more than a tune-up, an off-Broadway drill, for the more demanding performances that will be required of them during the lunch and dinner hours. "Customers aren't quite as tense in the morning as they are later on," says a senior waitress. "They want that first cup of coffee, and they want it fast, and we get it to them. But, generally, they haven't yet been whacked by the day." What's more, the morning crowd tends to spread itself across two or more hours, compared to the more condensed invasion of, say, the noon-hour crowd, which comes over the hill just before 12 and establishes a ninety-minute bivouac that occupies every available portion of the restaurant's ground, air and psychic space.

Afternoon shift. From left, waitresses Anne Makela, Eija Niivila, Rita Rintakangas, Melanie Bingham, and cashier Sinikka Ahtila.

If the battle metaphor wears thin at this point, it is because, unlike real armies, the respective forces here have come to the battlefield with the most positive and time-honoured of intentions—one to eat, the other to serve. "The most satisfying thing we do around here," says Tuula Granholm, "is to make the customers happy."

It is for happiness, then, that noon hour at the Hoito is a rampage of strategic survivalism; that aspersions and epithets are fired across the kitchen like bullets; and that every plate in sight and every corner of cooking surface is piled an inch deep in food, and headed for the boiling point. At times such as this, the cooks and waitresses are united in a pervasive low-key nattering, spiked every few minutes by a brief exchange of antipathies, mostly in Finnish, the working language of the restaurant, spoken by all but two of the 57 employees. "We say some pretty wild things to one another under stress," admits Arja Maki, who acknowledges that the backstage comments and grievances are a necessary valve on the inevitable build-up of tension. "We can't vent on the customers," she says, "so we do it on one another. But as soon as the rush is over, we're friends again, and we joke about how we can do this to one another."

Waitresses earn marginally lower wages than kitchen staff, but are compensated for both the shortfall and the strain of their work by the 30, 40, 50 dollars in tips that they are able to make in a day. While the waitresses are reluctant to talk about tipping, one did allow that the best haul she had taken in twenty-five years on staff was $105 on a single shift. Another claimed that the best tips come in the morning and evening, and yet another that, in the days before smoking was banned in the restaurant, smokers tipped better than non-smokers. The same woman explained to me that rectangular tables yield better tips than round ones—a notion greeted with high scepticism by waitress Eija Niivila, who earned $1.70 in tips during her first day on the job in 1972. By tradition, at the end of each shift, the waitresses give 10% of their tips to the busboys and busgirls.

When the lunch riot ends at about 1:30, and the dust settles, the restaurant enters a kind of doldrums, a recuperation period in which the shift changes, and the waitresses and cooks can eat their meals and smoke their cigarettes in relative tranquility. The food that comes out of the kitchen between 2 and 4 p.m. does not match in volume what came out in fifteen minutes during the noon hour.

As the afternoon ripens, however, the vitality of the place reconstitutes itself. By five o'clock, the contingent of waitresses is back up to six, the cooks and helpers are at their posts, and the first wave of diners has begun to arrive. Tonight's menu board features a ballot of gutpackers that includes Finnish sausage, pork chops, spaghetti, roast beef, roast pork, fried lake trout, and *kalakeitto*, a fish-lover's stew made from fish stock, potatoes, and chunks of salmon and trout. The table menu lists liver and onions, ham and T-bone steaks, *mojakka*, *suolakala*, Hoito burgers, omelettes, and of course the *sine qua non* of the restaurant, Finnish pancakes, tendered tonight with a choice of strawberry, raspberry or blueberry sauce.

Beginning at about 5:30, the backstage chorus rises gradually in volume and dissonance, until by six o'clock it is pretty much a reprise of the clattering ruck of the noon hour. Food is flying…and Finnish expletives. There are 110 diners in the seats, sixteen on the stairs, and, at any given moment, three or four rising from their table, tucking loonies and toonies beneath the edges of their well-visited plates.

And so it goes…until 6:45, or so, when, unnoticed at first, the equilibrium is tipped, and, for the first time in an hour, there are fewer customers arriving than leaving.

By 7:30, when the flames beneath the grill are doused, and all cooking ends, there are eight empty tables. Then a dozen. If there is beef or pork left in the steam table, and a little potato and salad, you can still get a meal. Until 8 o'clock.

Then it is over.

By 8:15, the last customers have left the restaurant. They are followed out promptly by the last waitress and cook, who have been ready to go for ten minutes. For both of them, the day has been long, but by no means the harshest of possibilities. "On any given day," says Arja Maki, "one of us finishes a shift saying 'I can't take it anymore. I'm leaving. That's it. It's over. Good-bye.' But next day, it's forgotten, and we're smiling again, happy to be back."

For Sirkka Ahola, with whom I entered the restaurant at 3:45 a.m., the day has been over for nearly nine hours. The last I saw of her, she was sitting at the staff table nursing a cup of coffee, a slice of pork and a little mound of coleslaw. She looked weary but contented as the kitchen rattled around her. She was eventually joined by 19-year-old Jenni Glad, a part-time student who normally toils as a waitress but on this day was being tutored in the craft of salad-making. Then came Eevi Savioja, whose presence at the table that day has become for me a lasting caricature of the bone-weary Hoito employee at the end of a shift. There she sat, in zenned-out exhaustion, wearing the wet rubber gloves in which she had recently been washing dishes, holding a salt fish sandwich in one hand, while a steaming cup of coffee waited poised in the other.

All but three of the Hoito's employees are women. Their ages span more than fifty years. They are daughters, mothers and

Cashier Kaija Heikkinen.

grandmothers, some from the same family. And yet any of them could tell you that, at work, they are not so much a ladder of generations, or an occupational hierarchy, as a sisterhood—nurturing, egalitarian and very hard working. As the restaurant nears its 80th anniversary, it is far from an exaggeration to say that the women who run the place today are an honourable embodiment both of its early ideals and its enduring name, which translated into English means "care."

"If you didn't care, I don't think you'd last long around here," says Anne Makela, an affable waitress who began work at the Hoito in 1980, at the age of twelve. Like many other employees, Anne has left and returned to the restaurant. "I went out to B.C. for a while," she says. "Then I went to Toronto to study fashion design and worked in the clothing business. Now I'm here again."

"When people quit," says Sirkka, "they always say they're never coming back. But they always do."

"The truth," says Arja Maki, "is that once you've worked here,

The Finn Hall
and Hoito
today.

a part of you never leaves." As she articulates these words, she picks up a coffee pot and pours a cup for an elderly gentleman who is seated in front of her at the counter.

"Which part would you be talking about?" the man says solemnly.

"The part that doesn't know any better," she laughs.

"You think you've got it bad," he says. "I can't stop coming, and I have to pay for it."

"How long have you been coming here?" I ask.

"Since 1932. I was eight years old. I sold papers on the corner. I used to come in to get warm—me and my dog. In those days there was always a dog or two in here. The food was wonderful. It still is. My name's John Mulholland, by the way."

We shake hands, and I ask John what he imagines the founders would think of the place today.

He scans the dining room, reflects on the question, and takes a fluttering sip of coffee. "Don't quote me on this," he says presently, "but they probably never imagined it would turn out as well as it has."

❖

Silver Islet

I visited the community of Silver Islet for the first time during the summer of 1991, while in Thunder Bay to teach a writing course at the now-defunct Curtis Summer School of the Arts, at Confederation College. That was several months before I moved to the Lakehead with my family, or even imagined such a move would take place—but I recall thinking at the time that if I ever got back to this tiny community on the windward edge of the Sibley Peninsula I would make certain to record my impressions of it, perhaps in the form of a travel-page feature or magazine article. Typically, I was impressed by the power and beauty of the landscape and lake—but equally, I think, by the paradox of that beauty: grandeur addictive and inspiring to its human inhabitants yet capable, in an hour of upheaval, of routing them, as it did to the settlers during the days of the legendary mine.

Human fragility was very much on my mind as I reread the piece recently and realized that, in the short time since it was written, no fewer than three of my sources—Ann Drynan, Bob Heise and Frances Hobson, each a devotee and fixture of the community—had passed on.

When the piece was published, I got comments on it that were about equally positive and negative. One gent told me that I'd portrayed Silver Islet as "a buncha nut cases," another that I'd captured the place "dead on."

It was certainly never my intention to seek out eccentricity during my preparations for the article. During my many visits to Silver Islet over the years, eccentricity has often, in fact, sought me out, and I feel I'd have been remiss not to report it as a vital thread in the community's existence. I have tried to report it in approximately the measure I found it—or it found me.

One of my supporters throughout, Tom Dyke, who spends about four months a year at Silver Islet, phoned me when the article appeared, told me that, in his opinion, I'd done an okay job, and that the piece was "98.3 per cent correct."

"What'd I get wrong?" I said, mildly perturbed.

"One-point-seven per cent," he said solemnly.

"Facts?" I said.

"Oh, no, no — just a few things about the spirit world."

"Like what?" I persisted.

"Trifles!" he said. "Nothing worth worrying about. Your facts are impeccable."

Here, then, are the impeccable facts...with minor distortions in the spirit world.

YOU DON'T HAVE TO KNOW the people of Silver Islet to appreciate their community on the north shore of Lake Superior. The place is one of the oldest summer settlements in the country, and the surpassing grandeur of its geography makes it one of the finest.

But to meet the inhabitants, at least a select few, is to add piquancy, a mildly hallucinogenic fix, to whatever else you might glean by, say, standing on the local public dock, leaning into a Force 7 westerly as it funnels down the channel between Burnt Island and the mainland. Or sitting on any of a dozen or so waterside verandas on a night in late July, sipping your favourite potion and listening to the loons as they interview themselves 50 metres offshore.

Or watching the slow cascade of stars, the greatest show on earth, as it slides over the horizon behind the Shaginash islands (better known locally as "the Shags").

For a taste of this incarnate piquancy, one would do well, for example, to meet Jack Drynan, a long-limbed septuagenarian with glo-white thatching and a passing resemblance to the great blue herons that occasionally wing their way overhead on their way to or from base camp. Among the avocations listed on Jack's calling card are: "dump inspector", "whiskey sampler", "chipmunk trainer", "dock watcher", and "thunderstorm commentator." This self-avowed "normal guy" has been spending summers at Silver Islet since, as one resident put it, "Shakespeare was a cowboy." He has held seances there, and has had psychic communication not only with former residents of the Islet but with extraterrestrial visitants — "which was *really* interesting," he confides.

Jack Drynan: "Whiskey sampler, lightning watcher, garbage dump inspector, chipmunk trainer..."

Silver Islet General Store and Tearoom today, viewed from the dock.

Meet his wife Ann, another longtime summer resident, who during the 1930s was paid 50 cents for every bear she could skin to provide chow for the local fox farm.... Or 36-year-old Nancy Saxberg, whose family runs the Silver Islet General Store and Tearoom, established in 1871 (and re-established several times since). Nancy is a photographer, artist, and exceptional restaurateur — certainly no flake. Yet she allows that, on an afternoon last summer, in the attic above the store, she felt a hand descend on her shoulder — an incorporeal hand as it turned out. For when she swung to acknowledge the unbidden advance, there was no one behind her, or even in sight.

When you arrive at Silver Islet for the first time, there is a sense that you are entering a rather rich, fragile dream, untranslatable into the rigid arithmetic that governs most of the planet.

The fragility is partly a matter of scale. At the tip of Sibley Peninsula near Thunder Bay, this historic summer settlement sits with its back to massive diabase cliffs, its front exposed to the ripsnorting winds and storms that regularly rage off Lake Superior. Even on calm days, in these parts, human settlement—humanity, period—tends to be dwarfed by the vast, icy indifference of the lake.

The fragility is equally a matter of time, time's passage, mortality. Just a kilometre or so offshore lies a forlorn little island from which the mainland community takes its name. One hundred and twenty years ago this tiny island was the site of the richest silver mine in the world—a glittering symbol of humanity's grandest designs. Today, there is no trace of what went on there, save a few underwater timbers and two small black holes in the lake bed, the mine's shafts, eerily visible from a boat or low-flying plane. Time and nature have swept away the rest.

As if the residents of Silver Islet needed a reminder of their place in the grand scheme, last winter a 400-kilo boulder tore itself loose from the cliff above one of the summer residences, where it had rested for a thousand centuries, and crashed through the building's roof and upper storey to the main floor.

Or was it an 800-kilo boulder?

History, even of relatively recent vintage, is not entirely fixed in these parts. It comes unstuck, lends itself to reinterpretation. Longtime summer resident Jim Cross is both quaint and direct in assessing the local revisionism: "Fifty per cent of what you hear around here is bullshit," he says solemnly.

"You tell a story at one end of Silver Islet," agrees Hugh Stevenson, another cottager, "and by the time it gets to the other end, it's a completely different story."

For anyone who has yet to get the gist of things, Silver Islet is not so much the *setting* for a story as a story unto itself, a constantly evolving narrative, whose authors and characters are one and the same, the inhabitants of the community. Some of them are factualists, some are not. Some are living, some dead. The history of the place is much less the dry bones of text and date than a multiplicity of spirits that inhabit this crag of rock, this log cabin, these ancient rooms above the store.

Nowhere is the spirit more concentrated than on the tiny offshore island where, in 1868, prospector Thomas Macfarlane found a silver vein of such size and purity that it stirred the blood of the mining industry around the world. Question was: How could you mine silver on a hunk of rock less than thirty metres long and wide, surrounded by frigid water and hammered by periodic gales? Winter on this exposed chip of real estate could freeze a man numb in minutes.

The challenge fell to an obsessive Irish mining engineer named William Frue who, with a crack unit of Michigan mining veterans, attacked the problem with militaristic verve. In a few months, working in weather that at times threatened their lives, these Victorian commandos installed massive timber cribwork around the entire island, and filled it with rock.

The expansion brought the islet to an area of nine acres, forty times its original size. Head frames, packing plants, and boarding houses sprouted on site. A shaft went down. Steam-powered pumps worked 24 hours a day to keep it dry.

A kilometre or so away, on shore, the remote tip of the Sibley Peninsula was transformed into a rattling company town just twenty-five kilometres by water from present-day Thunder Bay. The place included two churches, a saloon, a government office, a

The mine site offshore.

magnificent store, an assay office, an ore-processing plant, a warehouse, a blacksmith shop, a hotel, and a jail. Company officials lived in large frame homes along the waterfront, while married workmen and miners occupied tidy log houses constructed of local pine.

By 1872, the population stood at 500, making the settlement the largest on the north shore of Lake Superior. The twice-daily steamboat service that operated between Silver Islet and Port Arthur (now Thunder Bay) was the only way in and out between April and November. In winter, it was dogsled or horses or nothing. But with silver flowing in such abundance, few balked at the inconvenience. Miners were earning a munificent $2.25 a day, while the mine president and manager were paid an all but unaccountable $5,000 a year. Wealth was accruing to the shareholders in tens of thousands of dollars a month.

But despite speculation that the mine would be operating well into the 20th century, the grade of ore began to decrease during the mid-1870s. Silver prices dropped. Mining costs soared.

Then it was over.

When a barge carrying the winter's supply of coal for the water pumps got frozen in on the south shore of the lake in late 1883, water flooded the shafts. The mine shut down the following year, and attempts to reopen it in subsequent years met with marginal success at best.

The community was quickly deserted—although not for long.

"If you were living in Port Arthur or Fort William at the turn of the century, the thing to do on a Sunday afternoon was to get on a steam tug or a casual steamer and go out on the lake, perhaps to the nearby islands," says 79-year-old Stewart Webster, a retired Queen's University history professor and, by his own estimate, one of the oldest (corporeal) residents of contemporary Silver Islet. "If you wanted to go a little further, you came around the tip of the peninsula to the old ghost town."

According to Webster, those earliest day-trippers were eventually succeeded by more adventurous sojourners who chose to stay a week or more, setting up housekeeping in the abandoned company homes. Many of the squatters returned year after year to the same dwellings.

Enter the Lake Coast Trading Company, a local syndicate with an eye for profit and an outlandish plan for Silver Islet. In 1910, this group of callow hucksters succeeded in buying the resurrected ghost town in its entirety from the Nipigon Mining Company. Within months, they had surveyed it, divided it into lots, and laid out a plan for a resort that, according to their literature, would include a "Roller Coaster, Loop the Loop, Shute the Shutes, Miniature Railway, Figure Eight, and other such attractions."

The resort, they clamoured, would be the Lakehead's Coney Island. Squatters were offered first dibs on purchasing property, "then it was *Hurry, hurry, hurry! Get your lots while they last!*" says Webster. "My dad bought ours in 1911 and we built this cottage on it in 1921." Many of the lots included company houses and cabins from the mining days.

With the coming of World War I, however, the North American real estate boom that had fuelled local speculation collapsed, and the syndicate went broke—before it could fulfil its giddy dream.

"I dare say that by 1917," says Webster, "some who'd bought property were probably looking in the mirror and saying, 'Sucker! Coney Island, my neck! Where's the merry-go-round?' With the war on, they couldn't even *get* to Silver Islet!"

But the '20s brought a return to prosperity, and by 1931, a road had been opened, linking the summer community to what is now Thunder Bay, seventy kilometres away.

Parts of contemporary Silver Islet have gone virtually unchanged in the one hundred and twenty-five years since the silver boom began. The community as a whole maintains its original shape— a more-or-less single line of residences stretched out along more than a kilometre of shoreline and connected by a narrow road referred to locally as "the Avenue." Indeed, some of today's 150-odd cottage-owning families—"camp" owners as they're called in northwestern Ontario—are descendants of the original mine employees. Jim and Brenda Cross (husband and wife, as well as distant cousins) are the great-grandchildren of Captain James Cross, a millwright who worked for the mining company and was eventually appointed caretaker of the abandoned settlement

"The Avenue" at Silver Islet during the mining boom. The store is top centre.

when the mine closed. "I'm a double Cross," laughs Brenda, who is Silver Islet's unofficial archivist, having collected vast quantities of photos, clippings, and documents pertaining to the community's history.

It was Brenda and Jim's great-uncle Julian Cross who, during the 1930s and '40s, discovered that the living were not the only inhabitants of the burgeoning summer colony. A wealthy mining engineer with spectral tastes, Cross held regular seances in the cemetery and store at the Islet, often bringing guests from distant parts of the United States and Canada to join him in his nocturnal experiments. "He used to call for his wife at these things," says Brenda. "He'd say, 'Ida, old girl, are ya there? Can ya hear me?'" British writer Sir Arthur Conan Doyle attended one such gathering.

"They used to stretch out a piece of film in the darkness while they were summoning the spirits," says Jack Drynan. "When they got the film developed, they'd see all sorts of things—Indians, people who'd passed on. Once they saw a railway bridge."

"A lot of people out here don't believe in any of this supernatural stuff," says Jim Cross, leaving little doubt about his own predilections. And yet it would be difficult to find a resident who would deny that Silver Islet possesses a curious otherworldly energy—a kind of mystic voltage—that attracts and infects visitors and casts a lifelong spell on inhabitants.

"One big difference between this place and other summer communities," says Bob Heise, "is that people come here from all over North America: California, Florida, the Midwest states, Calgary, Ottawa, Toronto, Kingston. And of course lots from Thunder Bay. Many of them spent their childhood summers here, as I did, and they're drawn back year after year—it's like a magnet."

Heise and his wife Ann make their own 1,400-kilometre pilgrimage from Mississauga. Their summer home, a one hundred and twenty-five-year-old miner's cabin constructed of white pine logs, is considered by some to be Silver Islet's most meticulously preserved relic of the early years, with its 19th-century window panes and original kitchen table and benches. Some of the pine planks in the interior walls are fifty centimetres wide. "A while back I rechinked all the logs," says Heise, "and my neighbour said, 'Goodness, Bob, you certainly work hard to keep this place looking old.'"

The Heises' front door has been battered so extensively by storms and wind since its installation more than a century ago that its centre panels have been reduced to the thickness of shirt cardboard. When the mine was operating, someone used to walk up the Avenue in the middle of the night during the coldest months to make sure smoke was coming from the chimneys. If it wasn't, people could be freezing to death in their beds. "Nearly every day, I'm reminded in some way of the incredible winters, the terrible hardships, that the first families must have endured out here," says Heise.

Today, Silver Islet is all but deserted in winter, and even during summer it isn't everyone's idea of the New Jerusalem. "When we told our friends we'd bought a place out here, they reacted as if we'd gone crazy," says Thunder Bay resident Betty Evans who, with her husband Jack, spends summers in a subtly renovated version of the Heise cabin. "A lot of people simply can't stand the lack of protection from the storms and the open lake. Really, it can be *miserable* out here on a rough day—we just love it."

Still others are cowed by the absence of electricity and telephone lines. Or by the long, twisting road that snakes along the Sibley Peninsula on its way to Silver Islet from the Trans-Canada Highway.

"I'd be lying if I said I liked it at first," declares Debbie Matthews who came here thirteen years ago when she met her husband Tom, a scion of one of the colony's earliest families. "But I've certainly learned to appreciate it."

The Matthews and their children, who live in Thunder Bay, make a summer home of the original mine office, a lovingly preserved frame cottage clad in pine planks. "Over here," points Debbie, "is where the miners came through the building on payday to pick up their money."

Last summer the Matthews, among the community's last holdouts, broke with nearly a century of tradition and installed a propane lamp in their place. "We'd never used anything but kerosene," says Debbie. "I said to Tom, 'Let's at least get propane over the sink, so you can make sure you get everything off the dishes.'"

In enumerating Silver Islet's assets, Debbie speaks glowingly of the strong sense of togetherness that inspires the community.

"People whose families have been coming out here for decades tend to get pretty close—not just the adults, the kids, too. One particularly nice thing is that the kids acknowledge the older people, say hello, help them out."

It is indicative of the cohesiveness at Silver Islet that, in 1991, when a sign was posted announcing that Nancy Saxberg would take a community photo to celebrate the 120th anniversary of the local store, nearly everyone in the village at the time, nearly two hundred and fifty people, showed up at the appointed hour to have their picture snapped.

Anyone who pores over the resulting black-and-white photo will come across a radiantly ample gentleman situated smack in the middle of the crowd. He is Tom Dyke, and the very mention of his name brings us back to those "piquant" individuals one really ought to meet in order to get the full flavour of Silver Islet.

Dyke has been spending summers at the colony since he was a sprout during the early 1930s. He owns the 120-year-old home of the original mine carpentry foreman, and can be seen around the

Georgia Wilkins (3) and Jack Drynan (80-something) on the steps of Islet House, the Drynans' summer home on "the Avenue" at Silver Islet.

village wearing full khakis and a pith helmet. He ties the cuffs of his pants tight to his ankles with string and, for reasons of his own, will not walk on carpeting or sit on fabric of any sort.

Throughout the summer, Dyke loads his Chevy van with tourists and conducts whimsical historical tours of the community, replete with lyric commentary. Let's join him as he drives down the Avenue, the narrow roadway that separates the historic dwellings from Lake Superior. Over here is Islet House, once the home of steamer captain Nicholas Marin, and just up the way the long-defunct Gitchee-Gumee Hotel, now a rangy summer duplex.

This is the spot where Dyke and his mother were occasionally invited to tea by the wife of the owner of Dow Brewery. And here's the antiquated house house where the 400-kilo boulder—"the intruder" as Dyke puts it—crashed through.

Up here on the left is the tour leader's favourite local garden—"breathtaking," he exclaims—and a clump of pink Himalayan balsam, a member of the touch-me-not family, said to have been brought to the Islet from England by Cornish miners.

Here's "Old Glory", once the Methodist Church, now a summer home. High in its peak is a little balcony with a bell where, according to local lore, the preacher used to hold forth to the Indians in their canoes.

Swing the van around to see Powderhouse Rock, a tiny, treeless island on which the miners kept their explosives. And around again towards the former site of the mine president's house, to which the the president's wife "would bring her piano every summer from Detroit, so she could treat her guests to recitals."

Back to the other end of the settlement to the old jail, now part of one of the summer residences, then over to Surprise Lake, a "bottomless" volcanic crater, just 300 metres inland from Lake Superior. Here, ninety-kilo sturgeon are said to rise to the surface once a year in May.

Down the hill to the assay office and across the road to the community store, the hearty hub of Silver Islet, with its breezy hospitality and revitalized antique fittings. After a visit to the store's tearoom for corn chowder, fresh scones and thick slabs of blueberry pie, Dyke leads his charges up Point Road to the final stop on our tour, his own rather eccentric domain, the carpenter's house.

Islet historian Tom Dyke whose summer home, glimpsed here, was once the residence of the mine carpenter

Here his commentary becomes a kind of abstract poem, ranging across everything from the small miracle of his television reception (battery powered) to the contents of his kitchen cupboards (opened for inspection) to his immaculate bedroom upstairs (his pyjamas are hung wrinkle-free on wire hangers, suspended on the wall).

In the room behind the kitchen, Dyke is asked about the presence of a disused galvanized bathtub. Without hesitation, he responds that he'd happily put it outside, perhaps plant flowers in it, except that "the spirits would shoot it full of holes."

"The spirits?"

"The ghosts," he says frankly. "There are a lot of them around."

Like the living, they tend to come back to Silver Islet.

"It's an extraordinary place," muses Dyke.

A rich, fragile dream of a place.

And no one, living or dead, is likely to deny it.

Summertime Blues

One of the old-fashioned pleasures of moving to Thunder Bay in 1991 was that, after seventeen years of relative exile—in the Bahamas for a year, on the prairies for a dozen, in southern Ontario for four—I was back on a part of the planet where I could pick decent quantities of wild blueberries (what I miss up here are the fresh corn and peaches of southern Ontario.) Over the years, I had picked sporadically in Muskoka and had picked Saskatoon berries along the roadsides and marshes of the Manitoba Interlake. But in terms both of harvest and of spirit, those experiences were a timid match for the more primitive pleasure of getting out on a cut-over north of Thunder Bay on a morning in late August or early September, wandering the edge lands and logging roads, hearing the ravens, and speculating on the presence of bears, moose, foxes, wolves, lynx (a friend claims to have seen a cougar in such territory in 1994)…and of course picking berries.

People from southern Ontario, who are inclined to believe that winter up here begins around Labour Day, might wonder how it is that our blueberry season extends into early September, while theirs is pretty much over by the end of July. Suffice it to say that, with the short growing season, the berries don't even ripen here until mid or late August. Last fall, in Pukaskwa National Park near Marathon, where the moderating influence of Lake Superior can keep frosts at bay beyond Thanksgiving, I picked perfectly good berries in sheltered areas alongshore during the first week of October.

All of this notwithstanding, when I think of blueberries, I think not so much of northwestern Ontario as of Muskoka where I picked as a boy. I think, too, of my mother, whose enthusiasm for picking was matched by her affection for the rocky uplands near the family summer cabin at Torrance, where berries were always available by, say, the third week in July. My mother was born and grew up in the Muskoka area, at Bracebridge, and on a July day a few years before her death from Alzheimer's disease in 1988, I drove her out to the uplands and guided her gingerly across the mosses and rocks of the local blueberry lands, holding tight at times so that the wind wouldn't blow her away. We sat under a tree, and I picked her some berries which she consumed with pleasure. Such was the power of her identification with the rocks and vegetation, the sounds and smells of the patch, that, for a few minutes, the combined effect of these seemed to dispel the ravages of her disease (as certain triggers could), and we were able to converse quite normally, as we had not done for many months.

When I contracted to write the following piece for *Cottage Life* magazine, in 1994, the editor, my old friend Ann Vanderhoof, perhaps fearing that I would lapse into irredeemable nostalgia, implored me to include some "practical advice" for would-be blueberry pickers—where and when to find berries, and so on. But as I began to write, I realized I didn't actually know much about that sort of thing, at least in any scientific sense. I was shown where and when to pick by people such as my parents, who were shown by their own parents. My mother knew as much about blueberry picking as anybody I ever met, but could not have put together so much as a sentence on soil chemistry or the fine points of blueberry pollination. What's more, the particulars of picking vary widely from one part of the country to another.

While I have included some scientific-sounding advice on the whys and wherefores of the berry patch, my aim above all was to convey the spirit of the activity.

Blueberry picking has gone on in this area since human beings arrived here after the departure of the last glacier some ten thousand years ago. And if humanity and the wilderness survive, it may well go on for another ten thousand years.

THERE ARE ARGUMENTS to be made for the strawberry and raspberry; but in my own gustatory opinion—a bias derived from perhaps five million berries picked and processed—the tiny blueberry, *Vaccinium augustifolium*, is the queen of small fruit, the singer in the band.

Its name alone is simplicity verging on poetry. And its shape is a teensy echo of the planet itself—which, as any spaceman can tell you, is mostly blue. For those unfamiliar with the berry's aesthetics, its likeness appears, full hue, on the Canadian one-cent stamp.

It is on the palate, of course, that the little blue prodigy really comes to life. Biting into a mouthful of blueberries is (to rephrase our lesser pitchmen) a tactile as well as a taste sensation, each berry releasing its inky ambrosial load with a subtle pop, followed by a burst of muted tartness, then the inevitable rush of fruit sugar that evolves smartly onto the deeper taste buds, flushing sideways and backwards off the tongue and down the hatch.

I prefer my berries fresh-picked, straight into the kisser in handfuls, right in the blueberry patch. But I'll happily eat them from a bowl with milk; on Cheerios, Shreddies, Bran flakes; stewed (is there anything in the realm of culinary satisfaction quite like the smile of the stewed-blueberry eater?); reduced to jam, jelly, syrup; with ice cream or yoghurt; in pies and puddings; on cheesecake or flan; in pancakes; in muffins. I have devoured them with gusto in chutney, and on salads in the form of blueberry vinegar.

The act of picking blueberries is, in its own right, a weirdly transcendent experience, a gateway both to wisdom and to idiocy. No emotion is quite comparable, for instance, to the hateful, delicious masochism of carrying on too long—say into the fifth or sixth hour; the head aching from too much sun; the retinas imprinted with blue-dot psychedelia that will pursue you into the twitchy dreams of the wee hours; and the *knees*, the *hips*, the *back*, each by this time a manifest inkling of the galloping arthritis that will eventually catch up with you. And yet you keep on picking BECAUSE THERE ARE STILL BERRIES TO BE HAD, AND AS YET NO ONE IS SHOWING CLINICAL SIGNS OF HAVING DROPPED DEAD.

Similarly, what can compare to the hopeful, agonizing self-delusion that, perhaps, if you don't look at your basket or pail as

My mother, Norma Wilkins, was an avid blueberry picker all her life, particularly in the Clear Lake area of Muskoka where she is seen here during the 1930s.

you drop in the blueberries, or if you pick them into a cup and dump the cup as it fills, your basket will somehow be tricked into filling more quickly?

Or to the sensory vocabulary of the patch itself: the varying desiccation and swamp; the moss, rock, and lichen; the snapping pungency of the dry-wire twigs being consumed by the cook-fire; or the redeeming cool of the lake.

Or farther north, the furrowed forest-cuts left by the pulp-and-timber men (prime ground for blueberries); the ubiquitous black spruce; the Precambrian ravens and rock.

My great-grandmother, a four-and-a-half-foot tigress, thought nothing of putting up seventy or eighty quarts in late July. She stewed them in their own juices—no added water—because this was how it was done. I've been told that she once emerged onto the cottage porch at Clear Lake, carrying a quart sealer of freshly stewed berries. As she held them up for the family's inspection, declaring proudly that they contained "not one drop of water," the bottom fell out of the jar, and the berries hit the porch floor.

As kids during the '50s and early '60s we picked in the mossy uplands near the Connell railway siding at Torrance, Ontario, a few kilometres south of Bala. Recently, the horrormeister, David Cronenberg, shot the final scenes of his movie *Naked Lunch* on the site. All I could think about while watching the scenes was blueberries. It might please Cronenberg that, during the mid-'50s at Connell siding, I found a heavy metallic *something*—military green in colour and about the size and shape of a cucumber. I showed it to my mother who, believing it to be an unexploded mortar shell, ordered me to lay it gently on the nearby moss. It may still be there.

The berries, like the prospects for the future, were good during the '50s. On most trips we'd come home with at least a six-quart basket filled. Some days, my dad would pick a basketful himself. If there was a deficiency to his efforts, it was that he didn't 'pick clean,' and that the time he saved in not separating the stems and leaves from his pickings had to be made up later by my mother, who did it for him. My mother, I might add, once stared down a rattlesnake in the blueberry lands north-west of Gravenhurst, Ontario.

I had no comparisons for the seemingly bountiful harvests of those early years, until 1991, when I moved with my family to

Thunder Bay. Last summer, my wife and five-year-old and I picked *twelve* six-quart baskets in the timber clearings out along the Armstrong Highway north of the Lakehead. An acquaintance and his family picked a *hundred* baskets in two days near Ignace, Ontario. Bring on Cronenberg.

Our own picking left my favourite jeans permanently stained in the knees, my fingers a fragrant ghoulish purple. My wife, who was six months pregnant at the time, sat like Buddha amid the bushes, and slept like him on the back seat of the van as she felt the need.

The operative word for good berries in these parts is "lovely." Exceptional berries are "as big as grapes." It is pleasingly symmetrical that the grapes grown north of Superior—the lovingly tended few that make it to maturity—are the size of blueberries.

When the berries are *particularly* plentiful—20 or 30 to a clump—pickers speak of "milking" them from the bushes...as we never could in Muskoka.

A local friend picks with a blueberry rake, an ingenious comb-like contraption with a litre-sized reservoir that traps the berries while allowing the twigs, leaves, and pipsqueaks to fall through. You can buy such an implement, hand-made from sheet metal and solder, for $35 at Lauri's Hardware, a Finnish institution on Bay Street in Thunder Bay. Lauri himself told me that, at the current price of berries, a rake would pay for itself in one trip to the patch. I believed it, but didn't buy one—perhaps because, for me, the pleasure of picking is only marginally connected to the number of basketfuls I bring home. Certainly, I have little patience for people who say they wouldn't waste their time scrambling around in the wilderness—not to mention wasting gas on the highway—when they can buy a basket of berries for 20 or 25 dollars. You can buy all the elements in the human body for thirteen dollars from a chemical-supply catalogue. But it just ain't the same.

In my own arcane world, the only reason for *buying* blueberries would be that you couldn't get them any other way. And, of course, sometimes you can't—even if you spend your summers in areas where they grow. Because sometimes they *don't* grow.

I have heard seasoned pickers expound *ad tedium* on the whys and wherefores of good and bad blueberry years. A good year starts with a warm spring, followed by wet June and a sunny July. Or was it a dry June and wet July? Too much rain kills 'em dead. Or too much sun. A late frost can apparently do them in. And if there are no bees or blackflies, the plants don't get pollinated.

Whatever else is known about their comings and goings, a few things are certain: Blueberries will inhabit an area for several decades, then disappear and show up somewhere else. Sometimes they return to an area where they were once plentiful. Clearing a patch of forest will often bring berries. A forest fire, too, will bring them on. Blueberries are one of the first plants to regenerate in the scorched soil. They like their soil acidic.

If you don't find berries where you hoped to, look somewhere else. Ask other pickers. A boom year at Huntsville or Parry Sound can be a bust at Sudbury or Connell siding. And remember that no matter what the prevailing conditions in an area, there will be microhabitats that experience nothing of the rain, drought, frost, blackflies, or fire that affect the territory at large.

As a rule, a relatively mild spring, followed by a good mix of rain and sun, tends to produce berries.

But aspiring pickers should not be confused, much less impressed, by any of this pseudo-scientific speculation. A good year is not one in which the rains or sun or frost come in textbook proportions at precisely the right time; or the berries are as big as grapes or grapefruits; or can be milked off the bushes by couch potatoes.

As much as any food on God's menu, I love blueberries. But given the choice between the berries and the berry patch, I'll always take the patch, with its implied freedoms, its wilderness and wildlife. In fact, at the risk of uttering a pomposity, I submit that a good year for blueberries is one in which you enjoy the patch as much as the berries—and perhaps have the good fortune to fill your basket.

A *really* good year is one in which you *really* enjoy the patch... and get to eat blueberries on cereal and ice cream—and in pies and pancakes and muffins—for weeks if not months to come.

Keeper of the Boreal Craft Shop

In preparing this profile for *Canadian Geographic* during the autumn of 1993, I enjoyed three lengthy chats with Freda McDonald, one of the most artful and respected Native elders in northwestern Ontario, if not the country. During our first two meetings, she was good-natured but somewhat diffident—perhaps uncomfortable with my use of a tape recorder.

Then on a cool day in early October, she invited me to join her at the Indian encampment at Old Fort William, where she worked. Within minutes of my arrival, she led me into the encampment's winter wigwam, where we sat on the cushion of spruce boughs that lay on the floor. Warmed by a little smudge fire that we took turns feeding, she opened up, speaking in detail and with great feeling about her private life, in particular the tragic occurrences of her childhood. She spoke so solemnly and quietly at times that there were long stretches during which her voice left no decipherable impression on my tape recorder.

What she said was so vivid, however, that I remember years later her description, say, of being taken from her family as a girl and being dispatched with her sister to a hateful residential school many miles from her home in central Manitoba...of being deprived of her language and even her toys. An image sticks with me of the sisters playing secretly with a doll their father had made, knowing that if the nuns discovered their play, they would be punished and the doll confiscated, as it eventually was.

Today, there is a remarkable serenity about Freda—a soulful acceptance of the truth of who she is and of what her life has been about. Her immense antipathy toward injustice and insensitivity is expressed not in anger or bitterness but through the exemplification of a better, more peaceable, way of doing things. It has occurred to me a number of times that, in her commitment to truth and passivity—and to the therapeutic power of productive manual work—she is in the same philo-sophic tradition as Gandhi. For all of this, however, she is by no means solemn in temperament. Freda loves a good laugh. And a good smoke. She lit up several times in the wigwam as we talked that day, peeking out furtively to see if any visitors were coming (in her working role as a 19th-century Ojibwa woman, she could hardly be seen with a duMaurier cigarette in her mouth). I mentioned her smoking in the article, but the reference was cut, as perhaps out of sync with Freda's implied saintliness. To me, it was all part of the same story, and I have reinstated what was removed.

The profile is simply written, but, largely because of the depth and integrity of its subject, has always seemed to me to possess an added measure of heart.

WHEN FREDA MCDONALD was a child during the 1930s, her mother would occasionally get a hunger craving that could be satisfied only by the meat of a rather unlikely mammal. "She'd say 'I feel like eating porcupine,'" laughs Freda. "And my brothers and I would run off and find one and knock it out of its tree. But when we'd killed it I always felt sorry that it had to die, and I'd pet the poor thing. But we never wasted even a bit of it. We'd use the quills and hair in our crafts, and when we'd eaten we'd put the bones into the fire as an offering of thanks to the Creator."

Though brief, her tale offers a crystalline window on tradition-al Ojibwa values. Survival, economy and spirituality were insep-arable. Human nature and Mother Nature were members of the same family.

Freda McDonald's workplace—her "office" as she refers to it with a wink—is an encampment of birchbark wigwams on the banks of the Kaministiquia River a few kilometres southwest of Thunder Bay, Ontario. As offices go, the place is decidedly low-tech. Apart from the human voice, the most sophisticated means of on-site communication is a collection of deerskin drums that, when beaten, can be heard for some distance up and down the river. In summer, the place is air-conditioned by river breezes. The only warmth in winter comes from the poplar fires that burn in the

Shelters such as these were used by local Anishnabe for thousands of years prior to the 20th century.

cooking shelter or occasionally in the winter wigwam. Wood smoke drifts through the encampment like the ghosts of the ancient aboriginals who lived in the area thousands of years ago.

Some forty metres away, separated from the wigwams by a dense clump of poplar and spruce, stands Old Fort William, a painstaking reproduction of the furtrading fort that existed on the river in the early 1800s. The wigwam camp is a re-creation of the Native settlement that stood outside the fort at the time.

During the warmer months, camera-wielding tourists pore over the site, not so much having fun as exercising the self-conscious curiosity and bemusement that often result when cultures and mythologies collide. To bridge the cultural and historic gap, several native employees of the fort circulate through the encampment in period costume, answering questions, cooking wild rice or bannock, and tending to the maintenance of the site. As time permits, they craft replicas of baskets, tools and cooking implements that their forebears used as far back as 10,000 years ago, long before the flourishing of Athens or Rome, or the building of the Great Pyramids.

Freda McDonald is the most senior and venerated of these natives. She in an Ojibwa whose Scottish surname was acquired from her non-Native husband in 1948, just before she was expelled from the Fort Alexander Reserve in Manitoba for marrying a white man. The marriage also deprived her of her official Native status and, in turn, nearly three decades of contact with the culture she was born to in 1932. Though her status has long since been restored, she has never discarded the hateful document that signalled her disinheritance: "Deemed not to be an Indian," it declares in bold script.

The irony is that few native Canadians are more "Indian" than Freda. During the nineteen years since Old Fort William hired her to work in and to develop the native encampment, she has so steeped herself in the ways of her ancestors that today she is a kind of one-woman heritage site, a self-evolved encyclopedia of Ojibwa lore and values. Not only does she know the old culture, she practises and teaches it, patiently conveying its meaning and methods both to natives and to non-natives.

Most evidently, Freda is a master of traditional Ojibwa crafts, which are the focus of her frequent public workshops and her weekly classes through the Native Employment Opportunities Program in Thunder Bay. She can scrape and tan a moose hide, build a wigwam, make a rabbit robe or a pair of beaded moccasins. She can craft a birchbark pot so sound that it can be used to boil water. "Many people don't believe you can boil water in bark," she says quietly (she says everything quietly), "but I've known the technique since I saw my great-grandmother do it back at Fort Alexander." The trick, she explains, is to fold and fasten the birchbark so that it doesn't leak. "Then you suspend the container over smouldering coals so that it isn't in contact with open flame. If your coals are hot enough, and you have enough patience, eventually your water will boil." The scientific explanation of the phenomenon is that water cools the birchbark

Freda at work on a birch bark wigwam at Old Fort William during the
1980s.

by drawing heat from it. The water will boil at 100 degrees C, while the birchbark, like paper, will not ignite unless it reaches a temperature of more than 200 degrees C.

The materials of Freda's handiwork are an inventory of nature's boreal craft shop: spruce root, porcupine quills, sweetgrass, rabbit fur, owl and grouse feathers, spruce gum, sphagnum moss, bone, antlers, sinew, stone, moose and deer hide, plus the wood or bark of cedar, birch, spruce, aspen and ash. At times, she complements her supplies with manufactured items such as ribbons, coloured beads and wool felt, goods first seen by the Ojibwa some 250 years ago and quickly incorporated into their craft-making.

Among the more unusual raw materials employed by Freda and her associates are the rounded wooden burls that sometimes form on spruce trees where the bark has been damaged. Depending on their dimensions, these are hollowed out to form drinking vessels, water dippers, or bowls, some as big as basketballs in diameter. Today's Native craftspeople typically employ knives or chisels in bowl-making, but earlier generations burned into the wood with coals, then scraped away the charring to form the bowl's interior.

Freda's harvesting of the forests extends to edible plants, everything from berries, pin cherries and wild rice to Labrador tea and a variety of leaves, flowers and roots. "The early natives made ingenious use of whatever enabled them to survive, anything they could turn into tools, clothing, food, medicine or shelter," she says. "Culture wasn't art, it was survival."

Though Freda is happy to divulge any of the secrets of her craft-making or food gathering, she is reluctant to discuss the knowledge of traditional medicines passed down to her by her mother, grandmother and great-grandmother. "In the early days, the survival of the tribe depended on those medicines," she says, "and the knowledge was given only to those who were willing to take the responsibility that went with it." She says the natural cures worked well for the early natives until Europeans introduced diseases that were beyond the scope of herbs, roots and potions.

Freda is emphatic in pointing out that, in spite of the pressures to survive, her forebears took no more from nature than they could use and killed only the fish and game that they and their communities could eat. "Unlike people today," she says, "they wanted to be *part* of the balance of nature, not simply to dominate it. And they were faithful in their gratitude for what the Creator provided."

Freda, too, is faithful, both in her gratitude to the Maker and in her non-invasive use of nature's bounty. She reverently conveys her values to those she instructs. As a prelude to a recent workshop in birchbark basketry, she took a group of local women into a spruce bog west of Thunder Bay to gather spruce root for use as thread. Before proceeding, she offered an Ojibwa prayer of thanksgiving and made the traditional symbolic offering of tobacco at the base of a tree. Then she showed the women how to dig into the soil, locate the wire-thin surface roots and bring them up for harvesting. Spruce root can run fifteen metres in length and is as strong and supple as snare wire. "But you have to be careful to pull only the thin roots," cautions Freda. "If you pull a thick one, a tap root, you can damage a tree. And when you finish, you always put the surface moss back in place for the good of the remaining roots."

In the interest of both ecology and discretion, Freda and her co-workers at Old Fort William resist harming either fauna or flora in gathering their materials. Feathers, fur and quills come mostly from animals or birds that die on the highway or in the wilds, while much of the bark comes from trees that will be used for other purposes. But the ongoing production of artifacts at the camp is by no means restrained by such prudence. Over the years, the place has become a locus of living history replete with paddles, cradle boards, leather items, pelt stretchers, drums, lacrosse sticks, kitchen tools, ceremonial pipes, bowls, drinking vessels, fur pieces, and baskets of bark and woven willow. The wigwams are masterful assemblages of birchbark rectangles sewn together with spruce root and fastened to conical frames made of spruce poles.

Because of her age, Freda not longer participates in the heavy work of wigwam building, but her handiwork remains evident in the older wigwams and, indirectly, in the wigwams built by younger men and women whom she has instructed in the craft.

❖

On a cool morning in autumn, Freda sits with a visitor in the winter wigwam, the warmest and solidest structure in the encampment. Smoke from a poplar fire rises through the centre hole of the dwelling, and spruce boughs cover the floor to a depth of eight or ten centimetres. Freda explains that the spruce boughs are not only insulation from the ground and a comfortable mattress, but a natural deodorizer for the wigwam and a repellent for snakes, frogs and "other creepy crawlers" that might try to come inside. Poplar, she points out, is the preferred interior fuel because it burns cooler than birch or ash, produces minimal smoke and,

Freda McDonald today.

unlike resinous woods such as pine or spruce, does not throw sparks that might ignite the highly flammable surroundings.

As she sits by the fire, there is an almost mystic glow to Freda's countenance. She is slightly built, and her cap of greying hair crosses her forehead in fine, even bangs. Her smile radiates from every part of her face. Like her ancestors, she is devoted to tobacco—in the form of duMaurier cigarettes, which she consumes at a longshoreman's pace.

Among local natives, Freda is a respected elder, known not just for her cultural expertise but for her patience, modesty and wisdom. "You can go to her any time with your problems," says Mary Kuurila, an Ojibwa woman who has attended Freda's Wednesday night craft classes for several years. "She doesn't try to tell you what to do, and yet after you've spoken to her you *know* what to do. She's a true teacher, in that she directs you toward thinking and acting for yourself."

"It's the same thing with the crafts," says another of Freda's students and admirers, Bond Strand. "Rather than doing the work for you, she makes you struggle with it a bit, so that when you're done, you know what it's about. She's a very wise lady."

Sitting in the wigwam, Freda turns her attention to a large birchbark basket near the circle of stones that surrounds the fire. "People often tell me that the crafts look great," she says, "but they have no idea of the knowledge or effort behind them." The making of even a simple-looking basket can take several days, beginning with the collection of bark and spruce root, then the separation of the bark into layers and the laborious peeling of the root. "The cutting and stitching of the basket can take a day or two in itself," says Freda, "and another day or two if you decorate it with quills."

The traditional making of leather items—moccasins, mitts, beaded bags—is a more demanding process yet. While most of today's "traditional" Native leather products are made from commercially tanned hides, the historic method starts with the killing of, say, a moose or caribou, proceeds to the removal of all flesh, fat and membrane from from the interior of the hide, then the time-consuming scraping of every hair from the hide's exterior. "After soaking the hide," says Freda, "you mash the animal's brain into a paste and rub it into the hide." The brain contains emollients and, according to Freda, provides exactly the amount of paste required for the process. "Nature provides," she says. Subsequent steps include seasoning the hide in a small enclosure with smouldering tamarack punk (decayed, slow-burning wood), washing it, then stretching it for hours, by hand, over a fire, a process that requires several people and is intended to break the fibres and give the hide colour and a pleasant smoky odour. "Then there's all the work of cutting, stitching, beading and trimming whatever it is you're making," says Freda. "From start to finish it can take days and days."

With her profound knowledge of the old ways, Freda can look at an artifact from another era and, judging by the natural materials used, make a telling assessment of the environment in which the tribe that produced it lived. What's more, she can see *how* the tribe lived, the level of sophistication of its tools, skills and work habits. "If you know what you're looking for and use your imagination, you can get a sense of the whole relationship between the craftsperson and his world," she says.

In keeping with the Ojibwa notion that all aspects of a culture are interrelated, Freda sees craft-making not just as manual or historical but spiritual. "For me, the work is very therapeutic and centring. It's a healing thing."

Freda, as much as anyone, knows the importance of healing. At the age of five, she was taken from her reserve home and thrust into a residential school where for ten years she was deprived of her language, her community and, except during summers, her family. "It was very, very lonesome," she says. "I felt abandoned; I was heartbroken."

Freda's cultural disinheritance was sealed in 1948 with her marriage and subsequent expulsion from the reserve. Still teenagers, she and her husband began a peripatetic existence that, twenty-nine years later, would bring them and their seven children to Thunder Bay, where treatment was available for a disabled son.

Shortly after arriving, Freda learned that the recently constructed Old Fort William was seeking seamstresses for its costuming department. "I went out to the fort to apply," she says, "but when I told them my background they were more interested in employing me in the Indian encampment. In those days the

Freda with her sons in 1954.

camp was just a single wigwam in a clearing, hardly developed at all. But I took one look at it and knew that this was where I wanted to work. It was as if, after all those years in exile, I'd come home. A few days later, I started work as an Indian," she laughs.

Freda brought with her to the fort a dimly recalled knowledge of traditional crafts that she had acquired as a child through her mother, grandmother and great-grandmother. More importantly, she brought a willingness to learn. Over the years, by reading and studying artifacts—and by experimenting with different types of crafts—she taught herself what she knows today. "I immersed myself in the work and began gradually to reconnect with myself and my culture. It was like coming full circle to my childhood and starting from the place where I got lost."

Today, during her Wednesday night craft classes, Freda imparts the same sense of focus and reconnection that she herself has derived from her studies and her work in crafts. "Natives and non-Natives alike are hungry for this sort of renewal," she says. "Both cultures have lost their connection with the Great Spirit. They're caught up in greed and excess; they don't share." She reflects briefly and says, "Too many people have lost control of their lives; they don't do things for themselves anymore. My people were stopped from doing for themselves. They became totally dependent. My generation was the first to receive family allowance, social assistance. Before that we were independent."

Freda remembers the Sunday during her childhood when the local parish priest ordered every family on the reserve to apply for the newly introduced family allowance benefit of five dollars per child. The penalty for not applying was excommunication. "My dad didn't want to," she says, "but he was Catholic, so he signed the application form. I remember him saying, 'If I sign this, I'll lose control of my family.' That struck fear into me, even though I didn't know what he was talking about. Shortly after he started receiving family allowance, his kids were taken and put in boarding school."

On an optimistic note, Freda observes that the old ways, the self-reliance and spiritual awareness "seem to be coming back. Things are slowly getting straightened out."

Freda welcomes a visitor to Old Fort William.

As a complement to the work in leather, bark and beads at her weekly class, Freda often leads a healing or prayer circle. "For purification, we burn sweetgrass, tobacco, sage and cedar," she says. "We join hands and let one another know that we're not alone, that we need one another's strength and the strength of the Creator to carry on. We pray in Ojibwa—not a set prayer but according to our needs."

Not everyone is as receptive to Freda's work and leadership as those in her classes. "Some visitors to the encampment at the fort are very insensitive," she says. "They come with a Hollywood type Indian in mind; they whoop and laugh and make jokes. And sometimes I go up to them and say, 'Are you here to learn or to make fun of people?' That stops them short, and I say, 'Let me tell you about my culture.'"

And she tells them. And shows them.

And those who watch and listen—natives and non-natives— are richer and wiser because of it.

The Icy Adrenaline High

Apart from my usual silvery interest in making a living, I cannot recall the specifics of my motivation to write the following story. The suggestion may have come from photographer Lori Kiceluk, who took the photos that accompanied the story when it appeared in *Canadian Geographic* magazine…or from a conversation with Shaun Parent, the much-admired climber generally regarded as the founder of ice climbing in northern Ontario. I do recall that initially I was more interested in observing the sport than in participating in it. In fact, had I possessed so much as an inkling of its torturous physical demands, even at its simplest levels, I probably wouldn't have offered myself to it as a journalistic guinea pig.

As I note in the paragraphs to come, when I was half way up the ice fall to which I'd been matched, and was so thoroughly wasted that I wanted nothing more in the world than to quit, to get down, to crawl off into the woods and await the wolves, I was inspired to keep going by some irrational inner compulsion not to disappoint those who were witnessing and instructing my climb, among them my wife Betty and son Matt—the smile at the bottom of the ladder, as Henry Miller once put it. Betty and Matt had the faith of saints in my endeavours, and, in the light of their expectations, I inched my way up…and, in retrospect, am happy enough that I did. Even now, Matt, who was six at the time and is now nine, regards the day as one on which his old man did something—anything—of measurable value. Such was his take on my daffy heroics that on occasion he urges me still to return to the scene of my conquest, or to take up mountain climbing (a suggestion recently supplanted by a recommendation that, at age 48, I try out for the Chicago Bulls of the NBA).

One thing that pleases me particularly about this story is that it afforded me the opportunity to write, if briefly, about Shaun Parent, whom I admire for his vision and skills and survivalistic

55

spirit. He is one of two high-level athletes in Thunder Bay about whom I would one day like to write at greater length (the other being ski jumper Steve Collins). As the current story suggests, Shaun's c.v. reads like a script treatment for half a dozen episodes of *Mission Impossible* (he was contracted recently to do stunt work for the latest Batman film). For the past few years, he has spent the months from late spring until late fall in Peru, leading pack mules into remote areas of the Andes, to make geological assessments for Abitibi Price. He spends his winters, of course, climbing ice, promoting the sport he has made famous in this area and, indirectly, promoting the area itself.

L IKE MOST CANADIANS, I am on familiar terms with ice. Every autumn for several decades, I have watched it crystallize on local lakes and rivers. I have waited for it to melt in spring. I have pushed pucks, broomballs and curling stones across it, have skated on it and fished through it. I have scraped it (too often) from the windows of my car.

As a kid, I ate it in the form of icicles. I have sculpted it, slipped on it and plopped it into drinks.

But until April 12, 1994, it had never occurred to me to climb it. On that date, however, I joined a growing number of Canadians engaged in the extraordinary sport of ice climbing.

Question: How do you climb a waterfall?

Answer: Wait until it freezes.

Conceptually speaking, you then employ skills that fall somewhere between those of Spiderman and of the greased-pole climbers who used to compete at rural fairs.

Practically, you employ a range of implements—ice screws, ice axes, ice hooks, crampons and carabiners—several of which would double nicely as combat weapons. The ice axe, for example, is a high-tech hatchet on which the cutting edge has been reduced to a single serrated claw about a dozen centimetres long (I recalled as I held one for the first time that the psychotic killer in *The Seventh Deadly Sin* had stalked his victims with precisely such a tool).

The climber holds an axe in each hand, and drives them into the ice to serve as handholds. In an emergency, a properly driven axe will suspend the entire weight of a climber high on an ice face.

The equally menacing crampons are rigid steel cleats that fasten like a child's bobskates to a climber's boots. Each bears a double row of downward spikes, plus two or more front spikes, vicious buck teeth, that point straight forward and can be kicked into the ice to make a toehold.

With ice axes in my hands, crampons on my feet and a helmet on my head, I squinted up the 50-metre "ice-fall" that was to be my introduction to the sport. The name of the site, "Sycho Icycho," was an apt reflection both of my state of mind and of the sense of primitive giddiness afforded me by the instruments in my hands. For a veteran climber, this particular mass of ice near Orient Bay, about 140 kilometres north-east of Thunder Bay, would have represented little more than seven or eight minutes of brisk exercise. For me, it was a daunting, perhaps insurmountable, challenge.

Had it not been for the rope attached to my safety harness, I would have been far more concerned than I was about the consequences of falling off a 50-metre wall of ice. It is a given of the sport that climbers who ignore safety are not climbers for long. In my case, the rope—or belay, as such a safety device is called in climbing—extended from my safety harness up to an anchor at the top of the ice-fall and back down to where my partner held it ready to take up slack as I climbed.

With my pulse already racing and my adrenaline beginning to surge, I whacked one of my axes into the ice—and did nothing more than knock away a plate-sized slab of surface ice. Then another. When, finally, I had secured my axes, I raised a crampon, kicked into the ice, and took my first tentative step against gravity.

About fifteen metres up, breathing hard, I stood on a tiny ledge and rested. If I peeked over my left shoulder I could see the tip of Orient Bay, a spike-shaped southern extension of Lake Nipigon. Over my right shoulder were the boreal wilds of northwestern Ontario.

The Orient Bay area is ideally suited to ice climbing because, eons ago, a vast, elongated section of the earth's crust crashed downward between two fault lines, creating what is now referred

The author prior to climbing Sycho Icycho (the smiling man is the one who has not yet heard the bad news.)

to as Orient Bay Canyon. Over the ages, the canyon was widened by the weathering of its cliff faces—the Pijitawabik Palisades—and further enlarged during the Wisconsin glaciation, between 10,000 and 25,000 years ago, first by ice and then when the canyon provided a river bed for melted glacial water flowing south into what became Lake Superior.

Ice climbers are particularly enamoured of the canyon's east wall, a spectacular escarpment of fine-grained, slate-coloured basaltic diabase. In summer, within a few kilometres of Orient Bay, a hundred or more waterfalls pour over the palisades. In winter, each of them is a glistening cascade of ice.

My first view of those cascades had come six weeks prior to my inaugural climb, on a day of minus 30 degrees. As I drove up Highway 11, which runs along the base of the escarpment, I was distracted by a flash of bright orange, then one of purple, part way up the cliffs on a wall of ice. Seconds passed before it dawned on my that these were people. Climbers!

I watched through binoculars as the brightly attired daredevils picked their way skyward, the clinking of their axes echoing down the canyon like distant wind chimes. My initial impression was that they were either extremely hardy (it was, after all, -30 degrees) or they were nuts. Or both.

And now I was one of them, twenty metres up an ice wall, with my calves beginning to weaken and sweat soaking my inner clothes.

Although ice climbing is practised in other parts of Canada—notably the Rockies, Laurentians and Muskoka region of Ontario—Orient Bay is rapidly gaining a reputation as a prime playground for the sport. A 100-page ice climber's guide to Orient Bay and other sites north of Lake Superior was recently published in Madison, Wisconsin, and in February 1993, the ever-ebullient *Toronto Star* referred to the area as a "North American ice-climbing 'hot' spot."

"The climbs in the Rockies are longer," says Penticton climber Chris Gishler, a recent visitor to Orient Bay, "but you can only get to one of them in a day, if you can get to them at all. Here, you've got so many different climbs to choose from, each with its own character. And they're all accessible from Highway 11. You can do five or six in a day."

The development of ice climbing in the area is due in large part to the efforts of one man, Thunder Bay resident Shaun Parent. "He's a terrific climber, and he's done an awful lot for the sport," says fellow climber Julian Anfossi of Bowmanville, Ontario. "People come from all over this part of the country and from the United States—even from Europe—to climb with him and to learn from him."

Parent, a 36-year-old geologist and native of Windsor, Ontario, has the somewhat eccentric personality and demeanour that

Background, Shaun
Parent climbing an ice
ridge near Orient Bay.
Inset, Shaun in the
Nor'Wester Mountains
near Thunder Bay
Ontario.
Opposite, Shaun
climbing the Ribbon
of Death, near
Thunder Bay.

might be expected in a man who has devoted his life to scaling cliffs and frozen waterfalls. He dresses in bright, new-age clothes and, though balding on top, wears a six-inch braid down the nape of his neck. His round face is a perpetual study in curiosity.

An experienced mountaineer, Parent has undertaken climbs in Oman, Nepal, India, Thailand, the Canadian and American Rockies and the Peruvian Andes. He has never had a climbing accident, but has twice come close to losing his life during the days leading up to a climb. In 1984, in northern India, en route to Mount Indrasan, he was sleeping on top of a crowded bus when he was accidentally pitched to the roadside, breaking his shoulder, ribs and hand. "I was very lucky to survive," he says matter-of-factly.

Four years later, while leading an expedition in the Andes, he and his fellow climbers were awakened by the explosion of a grenade that had been tossed into their base camp. They were subsequently caught in a gun battle between Peruvian police and members of the *Sendero Luminoso*, the Shining Path Maoist guerrillas.

Parent's wife and frequent climbing partner, Joanne Murphy, has also suffered serious injury while preparing to climb. In early December 1992, prior to ascending an ice fall at Orient Bay, she was struck on the shoulder by a freak falling rock she describes as "the size of a loaf of bread." As a reminder of the occurrence— and of the importance of safety in climbing—she and Parent carry the rock to this day amid the piles of climbing equipment in the back of their Volkswagen van.

They also carry the memory of the unrecognized dangers that marked the founding of the sport in the Thunder Bay area in 1980. During the late winter that year, Parent, determined to gain experience for an upcoming climb in Nepal, persuaded his wife and a few friends to undertake a series of climbs on the ice of Kakabeka Falls, twenty-five kilometres west of Thunder Bay. As climbing continued at the site that winter and into the next, local Hydro officials began issuing warnings of the dangers involved. The flow of the river was unpredictable because of a dam upstream, they said, and the climbing site could be flooded unexpectedly, washing away hundreds of tonnes of ice, not to mention a few defenceless climbers.

Respectful of the warnings, but hooked by this time on ice climbing, Parent, Murphy and friends began the search for a safer habitat in which to practise their sport. ":What you have to understand," says Parent, "is that even a dozen years ago, there was very little ice climbing in Canada. There were no mapped or recognized sites. If you wanted to do it you had to create your own."

After several forays into the wilderness, Parent and a companion, Paul Dedi, "discovered" Orient Bay Canyon on February 21, 1981. Over the next ten weeks, they made numerous "first ascents" on ice falls in the area.

By late 1983, Parent had produced an elementary, hand-bound climbing guide to Orient Bay, and word had begun to spread. By 1986, climbers were coming to the area from Manitoba, southern Ontario, Minnesota, Michigan, Illinois and Wisconsin.

In 1988, Parent founded a guiding service for climbers and began offering regular instruction in the sport. At about that time, he also initiated a modest ice-climbing festival, called Ice Fest, which to this day is the only one of its kind in North America. Originally based in Beardmore, north of Orient Bay, the festival is now held in Nipigon, twenty-five kilometres to the south, and attracts scores of climbers from Canada and the U.S. "Because there are only a few thousand of us doing it," says Parent, "there's still a real sense of excitement and discovery. People like to get together not just to climb but to exchange ideas and techniques."

One of Parent's current projects is to get more teenagers climbing. "They're the future of the sport," he says "and they're certainly better off out here than in the video arcades."

Last winter, at the request of native councillors at the Rocky Bay Reserve on Lake Nipigon, Parent introduced a group of what he calls "problem teenagers" to ice climbing. "People back at the reserve couldn't believe what a difference it made in them," says Joanne Murphy. "It really improved their self-esteem and the way they interacted with one another."

Now, as I reach the 25-metre point in my climb, I find my own self-esteem becoming a trifle frayed. Below me, Parent is patiently calling out instructions: Keep my heels lower! Swing my axes from the elbow, not the shoulder. His encouragements notwithstanding, I have begun to have serious reservations about what I'm doing. Ice climbing is *very hard work* for a guy of middling years in, at best, middling shape. As the strength ebbs from my wrists and shoulders and calves, a voice within utters increasingly shrill regrets over the months of push-ups I've neglected to do, the kilometres I haven't jogged, the barbells I haven't lifted. I have, in fact, developed a low-grade case of what climbers call "sewing-machine leg"—a state in which the thigh and calf muscles are so exhausted that the entire leg begins to tremble involuntarily, as if working the treadle on an old-fashioned sewing machine.

What's more, I am fiercely thirsty. As I stop yet again to rest, I gnaw into a bit of loose snow on the ice wall in front of my face. I wolf it down and go for more. I glance skyward at the metres yet to conquer, and my inner voice shifts from regret to acute self-doubt: Why on earth am I doing this?

Why does anybody do this?

Shaun Parent instructing a climbing class.

A month earlier, at the ice climbing festival in Nipigon, I had put this very question to a number of experienced climbers. And, to a person, they acknowledged that, beyond the simple pleasures of being in the wilderness and getting exercise, they cherished the sense of accomplishment and elation—one climber used the word "euphoria"—that comes with getting to the top. "It's such an intense, sudden release," said Chris Gishler.

Mandy Dixon of Thunder Bay, who described herself as "a bit of an adrenaline junky," said she liked the thrill, even the risk, involved in climbing. "Up there on the ice," Gishler elaborated, "you can get yourself into some tight scrapes. Part of the game is getting out of them in a calm, rational way. It's a bit like meditating, a form of controlling your emotions, of not panicking."

Julian Anfossi listed "the look" of the ice among the sport's pleasures. "Each ice fall is so different, and they keep changing, like evolving sculptures. It's a clean sport, too," he noted. "It doesn't damage the environment or leave anything behind. When the ice goes in the spring, there's no trace that you've ever been there."

Shaun Parent draws an environmental comparison between ice climbing and rock climbing, a sport in which participants have been known to scar rock faces and damage delicate ecosystems. "Rock climbers will often cut away trees and plants for access to their routes," he says. "Not long ago, on the Niagara Escarpment, tests were done on cedars that climbers had damaged or cut, and these trees were discovered to be more than 200 years old."

"In purely recreational terms," said Anfossi, "there's a real sense of freedom on ice that you can't get on rock. Ice climbers can go anywhere—up, down, sideways, wherever they choose to plant their axes and crampons. In rock climbing you have to go where the rock dictates."

Asked if there is anything climbers *don't* like about their sport, Robin Sare, a Thunder Bay dentist, was quick to mention the intense cold in which ice climbing is often undertaken. "Your hands are above your head for the most part," he says, "and the heart wasn't meant to pump blood up there. It doesn't matter what you wear, your hands just get *so cold*." For that reason, most climbers prefer spring climbing, which, in the forests of northern Ontario, can go on into late April and early May.

"Ice climbing gives you a great sense of personal accomplishment," says Illinois resident Nancy Richards, who climbed recently at Orient Bay. "Yet it's also nice to be a link in the chain. When I'm handling the belay (the safety rope), the person up top trusts me with his or her life, which is very gratifying. And the sport is not gender specific. I've just started climbing, and the people make dispensations for me, but it's not because I'm a woman. It's because I'm new."

"That's one of the true beauties of it," says Joanne Murphy. "Even a new climber can make it to the top. He or she may be amateurish in the moves, but it can be done."

Indeed, my own amateurish moves have now taken me to within a couple of metres of Sycho Icycho's summit. And as I take my last torturous steps upward, I undergo an extraordinary psychological transformation. Under no other stimulus than the fact that I have made it to the top, or almost made it, my exhaustion and anxiety turn suddenly to a powerful amalgam of energy and elation. A bag of adrenaline seems to burst in my chest, and I virtually spring up the last few steps onto the little shelf of ice where the belay anchor is planted. I crouch there, attempting to catch my breath. As my adrenaline dissipates, I am able to appreciate the heralded sense of euphoria that comes of reaching the pinnacle. Drained to the core, however, I can bring myself to do nothing more than stretch out flat on the ice shelf and stare at the sky, my heart banging at about 180 beats a minute. Reminded of my thirst, I pull my glove off, snatch a fistful of crunched ice and stuff it into my mouth.

As I bask in my modest achievement, a raven soars out above me, circles ceremoniously, and drifts into the woods.

Eventually, I raise myself, dig in my axes, and, with a glance up the canyon to Orient Bay, ease myself over the edge.

The Practice of Paradise

As a child of six or seven, I knew two Finlanders: Auni Ikivalko, a friend of my mother's, who occasionally came to visit us from, I think, Toronto, and Kelvi Aspila, a student at McKenzie High School in Deep River, Ontario, where my father was the English teacher. I knew nothing about Finland or Finns, but as a kid who enjoyed language, I liked the sound of those rolling, euphonious names. "Eek-a-vollko" and "As-peeel-a," we used to say, entirely unaffected by notions of correct pronunciation.

As international hockey proliferated during the 1970s and '80s, my awareness of the Finns grew, although not by much—they were good hockey players! The best came to play in our leagues. In my ignorance of everything else about their backgrounds, I still enjoyed their names: Jari Kurri, Essa Tikkanen, Velli-Pekka Ketola.

Velli-Pekka Ketola!

It is often said that there are more Finns in Thunder Bay than anywhere outside of Finland. But I read recently it isn't so—Stockholm has more. There are, nevertheless, thousands of them in the Thunder Bay area, and when I moved to the Lakehead with my family in 1991 I gained an immediate appreciation of their (new-world) culture and karma. Within a week of our arrival we had adopted the venerable Hoito restaurant as a kind of home away from home. We made Finnish friends, with whom we socialize, work and play—we share their saunas and summer homes and cuisine. Our diet, thanks in part to the Hoito, is a repertory menu of *suolakala*, *viili*, *mojaka*, *hernakiito*, and Finnish rice pudding. I often eat a bowl of *kalakiito*, a fish stew that reminds me of a dish my mother used to make on Christmas Eve. My wife Betty bakes *pulla* like a Finn, and our kids will eat no pancakes other than the Finnish variety.

And still the names assert their peculiar euphonic charm: Koivu, Nikkila, Kukko, Kouhi, Toivanen, Leppanen, Poutanen, Sarkka, Syppila. As Kitty Kukko observes in the upcoming essay, "If you want to find the Finns, look for the vowels."

Otherwise, look in the sauna, the sanctified sweat box in which the primordial memory of the culture is most tangibly preserved. The sauna, let it be said, is where Finns hang out.

ON A FRIDAY AFTERNOON last June at about 3 o'clock, David Ranta shut down his computer, bid a dismissive *hei vaan* to the work week and abandoned his engineering office on the second floor of the family home on College Street in Thunder Bay. Ten minutes later, he was standing at the counter of the European Deli, a Finnish butcher and gourmet shop on Carrick Street. He bought a half-metre curl of *lenkki makkarra*, better known locally as "sauna sausage," and a slab of high-calorie coffee bread or *pulla*, a Finnish staple laced with cardamom and, thereby, smelling faintly of spruce boughs.

Then he headed out Hodder Avenue in the direction of his favourite place on earth.

David is a second-generation Canadian of Finnish descent. This means, among other things, that he speaks a modicum of Finnish, drinks precociously strong coffee (the national elixir of Finland), and shares with his countrymen a passion for the outdoors that runs as deep and green as the forests of Finland...which are said to bear an uncanny resemblance to the boreal forests of northwestern Ontario.

It also means, that like hundreds of other Finlanders in the Thunder Bay area, he maintains a summer cottage on one of the many lakes and rivers within an hour's drive of this city of 114,000. In these parts, however, he wouldn't dare call such a dwelling a cottage—"cottages," as any Lakehead resident can tell you, are the privileged preserve of soft-skinned urbanites from southern Ontario. Up here, they're called "camps"—that's anything from a one-room swamp shack to a luxury retreat on the shores of Lake Superior. The terminology hearkens to the days when the wives of lakehead loggers, the majority of them Finnish, would gather up the kids and join their husbands for the summer at any of the scores of bush camps that stoked the region's economy and spirit.

And "camp" is where David is headed as we follow him up Copenhagen Road to a point about ten kilometres north-west of town. Here, a rutted laneway, narrowed by saplings and ferns, leaves the main road and tunnels north through the forest to the four-room cabin bequeathed to David by his grandmother during the early 1980s. Located on the north branch of the Current River, the place is a spit in the eye of the late 20th century: no electricity, no indoor facilities, no double glass. And yet in its Luddite charms—solitude, sauna, unviolated riverbank—David and his family would seem to have found much of what they need to know of paradise. And, by extension, of the *practice* of paradise, the quotidian maintenance that Milton described diligently in his famous poems on the subject and without which not even the simplest camps or cottages could hope to survive.

It is with the latter in mind that David sets about preparing for the arrival of his wife Margot, their children, and a family of guests in a little more than an hour. He sweeps the verandah, shovels up a mess of old shingles that have been tossed from the roof, fetches water from the river, and puts a double-strength pot of coffee on the propane stove.

He then enacts a ritual that, for centuries, has been at the core of Finnish culture. He gathers an armload of spruce off the woodpile, takes it into the sauna, and lays it carefully in the handmade stove.

And lights it.

Like all saunas before they are heated, the interior of this one is clammy and uninspired. But in the presence of fire it comes alive with the fragrance of woodsmoke and cedar…and, as the minutes pass, with a seductive cottony warmth.

Eventually, with the temperature nudging 80 degrees Celsius and the water in the stove reservoir beginning to vaporize—and with the family and guests just arrived—David strings a line above the stove and dangles the sauna sausage within inches of the stove rocks to cook. When the skin splits in about 30 minutes, it will be done.

In the meantime, in various states of undress—towels, bathing

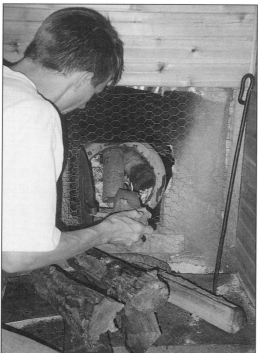

Above. Dave Ranta gathering wood outside the sauna at the family camp on the Current River near Thunder Bay. Left. Stoking the sauna stove.

suits, birthday suits—everybody piles in, adults on the top bench where the heat is greatest, kids down below.

Forty minutes later, dewy and squinting, they stagger out, one or two at a time, down the steps to the river for a plunge. Then it's back up to the sauna for a lather and rinse under stove water that by now is scalding and must be tempered with water from the river.

It would be difficult to overstate the centrality of the outdoor sauna to Finnish camp life: it is hygiene, grooming, social ritual, spiritual and physical restorative—some might say Finnish fetish or self-psychiatric hideaway. Or even cuisine. "And it's not always certain where one part ends and the other begins," notes Ralph Poutanen who, with his Swedish wife Marion, owns a sauna (and, incidentally, a camp) north of Thunder Bay on Hawkeye Lake. "What *is* certain," says Ralph, "is that if there is no sauna at a Finnish camp, something's terribly wrong."

Not that such blights on the cultural code can't be set right. When, in 1992, Kal Nikkila and his family bought the dilapidated Bungalow Camp, a one-time luxury fishing resort built by the CNR during the 1920s on Lake Helen, near Nipigon, they were decidedly aware that there was no sauna on the thirty-building site. "Our very first job—our *very first*—was to convert the old wash house into a sauna," smiles the Thunder Bay businessman, who over the past three years has led a painstaking restoration of the resort. "You could tell the place wasn't built by Finns!"

The primacy of the sauna is such that it was traditionally the first building Finnish families would construct on a rural or lakeside lot. "They'd live in it while they were clearing land and putting up their camp or homestead," says Arnold Koivu, who for three decades has camped with his family on One Island Lake near Thunder Bay. "They didn't have much room, but they at least had warmth and a place to cook and stay clean."

Arnold's wife Eila explains that, during the early years of Finnish settlement in the area, children were often born in the sauna. "And they saw a lot of it from that point forward," she laughs. "That's where the heat and the hot water were."

Eila Langen who camps with her husband Eino at nearby Two

Friends on the lane into Ranta's camp: (l. to r.) Malcolm Ranta, Matt, Eden and Georgia Wilkins, and Matti Ranta.

Island Lake recalls that, during summer, when her own children were young, she and Eino would light the sauna first thing in the morning and keep it going right through until after dark. "I'd use the water for washing dishes, for clothes, for any sort of cleaning—the men would use it for shaving. The kids were in and out of the lake all day—then into the sauna to warm up. With the cold lakes up here, you really can't swim or water-ski much at the beginning or end of the season if you can't get warm in a sauna."

The Langens' son Gary, who camps with his family next door, touts the sauna both as a natural narcotic, guaranteed to put children to sleep at the end of the day, and as a balm for insect bites which, in June in northwestern Ontario, can infect exposed skin with the ferocity of a Biblical pestilence. "The heat opens up the pores and just seems to suck the poison right out," he says. "The bites don't swell or itch at all."

There is a titillating symmetry to the notion that, inasmuch as babies were at one time born in saunas, some may also have been conceived in them. And may still be. "When we were in high school and university," admits an area camp owner who prefers his comments on the subject to remain anonymous, "I remember guys and their girlfriends would drive out to their parents' camps during the cold months, fire up the sauna and nestle in for a good sweat."

Guys on their own were apparently more competitive in their sweat-inducing activities. "My buddies and I used to see who could take the sauna the hottest," says David Ranta. "It was a macho thing. We'd be in there with the temperature up around a hundred degrees centigrade, and one of us would throw a cup of water on the rocks. Then it was the other guy's turn to throw a cup—and so on, back and forth, until one guy couldn't take the heat anymore, and he wouldn't throw, and the first guy was the winner."

According to Ranta, a civil engineer who professes to like his saunas "boiling hot," the common practice of applying water to sauna stones does not actually raise the ambient temperature but creates vapour which conducts heat directly to the skin, making the surroundings *seem* hotter.

For those who use their camps during winter, to cross-country ski, for example, the sauna holds a particular appeal. "There's nothing quite like it when you're freezing your rear end off after being outdoors!" says Raymond Kukko, who during the 1950s was a competitive downhill skier and now lives year-round with his wife Kitty at their camp on Timmus Lake north-west of the Lakehead. Ray, however, has little use for the legendary winter practice of rolling in the snow as an antidote to the sauna's prodigious heat. "As far as I'm concerned, it's a stunt," he says. "I did it once as a kid, and I never did it again. Once Kitty tried it, and the shock hit her and she couldn't move. I had to pull her out of the snowbank. Of course, she's Irish, not Finnish," he laughs.

Like so many Finns in the Thunder Bay area, Ray is descended from immigrants who arrived in the Lakehead during the early years of the century, bringing little more than the tools and skills that had sustained them in the forests outside Helsinki or Oulu, or in Finland's myriad northern villages. They made their stake as loggers and sawyers and carpenters in the bush north of Lake Superior. "That's where the jobs were," says Ralph Poutanen, "but that's where their hearts were, too. Any Finn would rather be outdoors in the bush than in the mines or factories."

Today, the children and grandchildren of those immigrants— and thousands more who have arrived since—make a population of some 15,000 in the Thunder Bay area, the largest aggregation of Finns outside Scandinavia.

While the early years and Depression were difficult for the Finnish community, the years after World War II brought a degree of prosperity, and hundreds of local Finns exercised their ancestral preference for the outdoors by buying available Crown land on nearby lakes and rivers. That is why, today, north and west of the Lakehead, the gravel roads that lead into, say, Trout Lake, Island Lake, One Island Lake, Hawkeye Lake, Surprise Lake, Warnica and Howcum lakes are festooned with signs bearing names such as Nieminen, Kuusisto, Saasio, Kouhi, Toivonen, Kivisto, Nisula, Wainio, Leppanen, Kivinen, Nikkila, Wuorinen, Maki, and so on. "You can always tell where the Finlanders are," says Kitty Kukko. "Just look for the vowels."

"And if you can't tell from the road, you can tell from the water," says Ray Kukko, referring to the Finnish tradition of

Kitty and Ray Kukko emerging from the sauna at Timmus Lake with their granddaughters (l. to r.) Kathleen, Hannah, Tessie, and Alexandra Naroski.

building saunas within a metre or two of the shoreline. In the Thunder Bay area, it is not uncommon to see as many as half a dozen of them—miniature houses with erect chimneys and impeccable woodpiles—in a row on neighbouring camp lots. "If you didn't know better," says poet Elizabeth Kouhi who for twenty years has camped with her family on Warnica Lake, "you'd think you'd come upon a community of gnomes."

While the sauna is the most conspicuous feature of Finnish camp life, it is by no means the extent of the cultural legacy represented by the camps. Asked about that legacy, Kal Nikkila reflects for a moment and ventures that the most enduring feature of Finnish camp life—the sustaining feature—is not physical but psychological, the extraordinary passion of the Finns for the outdoors, for the woods and waters. "In the broadest sense, that's what camp is to them," he says, "a way of getting close to the bush and the lakes."

"It's not that other cultures *don't* love the outdoors," observes David Ranta. "They do—it could be prairie, marshes, mountains, desert, whatever. It's just that in Finland, by definition, the outdoors is the forest, so that's what the Finns have grown to love— they're boaters and fishermen and berry pickers, same as camp owners here. There are forests right outside Helsinki."

The national concern for the outdoors is such that many Finnish businesses and factories shut down for weeks during the summer so that all their employees will be able to get to the lakes at the peak of the season.

"Finns love the *solitude* of camp life," says Kal Nikkila. "It's in the blood, from centuries of life in the forest. Listen to the music of Sibelius—you can hear the Finnish temperament in it, the reflectiveness, the need to be alone."

"I consider trees a stimulus to the spirit," says Elizabeth Kouhi, seeming to confirm the meditational link between the forest and the Finnish temperament. "Most Finns don't agree with me on this, but at our place we hate to cut a tree down. That's why we've never cleared our land; we want bush not park." The simple, attractive camp where Elizabeth and her husband George spend summers, often in the company of their children and grandchildren, is indeed well shaded by unpruned spruce and balsam. Given the opportunity to get hydro several years ago, the Kouhis refused, partly on the grounds that running the line from the main road to the camp would entail the loss of too many trees. "I like to think of Finlanders as essentially Eastern in spirit, very introspective," says Elizabeth. "Unfortunately, the seven hundred years they spent under the Swedes, from about 1100 to 1800, tended to Westernize them. So you get those like me, who love the forest for its own mysterious order and those who want to clear it back to create an order that suits their camps.... But I'm sure we're each happy in our own way."

Elizabeth's affinity for the wilds draws her regularly to her outdoor kitchen, where she often has a coffee pot brewing on the wood-burning cast-iron range—or occasionally a pot of *Mojakka*, a robust Finnish stew that combines varying proportions of beef, potatoes, turnips, carrots and celery. The hard work of logging and lumbering is done at a distance these days, but Elizabeth acknowledges that camp life in the boreal outdoors can still stimulate the Finnish appetite for traditional dishes of the sort that were once high-calorie fuel for bush workers both here and back home. To drop in for breakfast at Eila and Arnold Koivus', for example, invariably means stacks of floppy Finnish pancakes, rich in egg and milk and served with blueberry or raspberry preserves. Lunch at Eila and Eino Langens' can mean fresh-baked *pulla* or coffee bread. And a visitor to Kitty and Ray Kukkos' might well be treated to Kitty's homemade *suolakala* , salted, uncooked trout from local lakes and streams.

And knock-out coffee.

Like traditional cuisine, the Finnish passion for woodworking and carpentry also finds expression in the rustic nature of camp life. "*Finns love wood*," says Ralph Poutanen. "Give 'em some logs or a pile of two-by-fours and a saw—even a little chunk of cedar and a pen knife— anything to make something out of, and they're happy. Then again, go back a hundred years, and you're at a point where a lot of Finlanders had nothing *but* wood to make anything out of. The instinct for it flows right down through the generations."

Even today, it would be difficult to find a local Finn whose parents or grandparents were not in some way dependent on wood for their livelihoods—whether cutting trees, sawing them into lumber, or refining that lumber into buildings or furniture. Ray Kukko's grandfathers were, respectively, a logger and a carpenter at the Port Arthur shipyards. Arnold Koivu and Kal Nikkila's fathers worked in neighbouring bush camps, where their mothers were cooks. Eila Langen's father owned a rural timber cutting and lumber operation in Lappe, near Thunder Bay.

"Very seldom will you find a Finn hiring anybody to do construction on his camp," says Arnold Koivu, who, as a boy, learned carpentry from his dad and worked with him to build the family camp during the 1960s.

Ray Kukko built his first camp as a twelve-year-old, deep in the bush at Trowbridge Falls, just north of Thunder Bay. "We made it out of logs," he says. "But we cut them and hauled them from a long way away, so that nobody'd discover stumps and know where we were. My buddies and I slept in the thing winter and summer."

Kal Nikkila, too, began early, using what he calls "grown-up tools," including an ax, by the time he was six years old. "My dad made me a little bucksaw that I still have hanging in the sauna at home."

Last summer, Kal and his family applied the final touches to the restoration of the capacious main lodge at Bungalow Camp, the old CN resort at Nipigon. The floors and woodwork, mostly B.C. fir, have been meticulously reworked and finished, and throughout the place the Nikkilas have added Finnish touches such as a 12-foot dining table custom-made from jack pine, and birch panelling and hand-hewn towel racks and fittings in the kitchen.

The interiors of many local Finn camps are lined in pine or cedar. The furniture tends to pine, spruce and fir. But in most camps there is also a range of fixtures and artifacts that bear a more personal testimony to the Finnish affinity for wood. At Kukkos', it can be found, among other places, in Ray's hand-crafted spiral staircase, and at Langens' in a collection of Eino's father's bird carvings. At Koivus' it's in the coffee table, hand cut by Arnold and his dad from the trunk of a giant birch.

Or it's in the sanctuary itself—in the care that, at, say, Koivus' or Poutanens' or Gary Langen's, has gone into the building of the

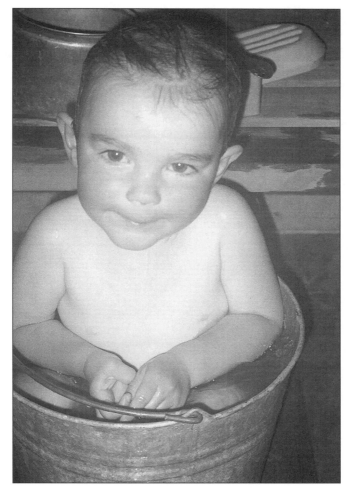

Eden Wilkins keeping her cool in Ranta's sauna.

sauna: the tight cedar planking and mitred corners, the rustic door handles and exterior cedar shakes. It's in the effort represented by the woodpile.

"Then there are saunas like ours, just the plainest little shacks," says Elizabeth Kouhi.

"Once the heat's up and the people are inside, it doesn't matter what a sauna looks like," says David Ranta.

Which brings us happily back to where we started, at the Rantas' camp on the north branch of the Current River. There, the sauna sausage is cooked, the coffee is thick, and the *pulla* is sliced and buttered. And it's all been transported to where supper is to be served at the picnic table in the clearing up the hill.

But for a minute or two, David remains in the sauna, reflective and relaxed. He reaches for a dipper of water, throws it on the stones and inhales the steam…and exhales it. "This is what I've always loved best about camp," he says quietly. "An hour in the sauna, and the cares just seem to dissolve. I sometimes come out for no other reason than to have a sauna." He glances out the tiny back window into dense boreal forest. "It's a world," he muses. "Could be Finland." But before his musings take root, the door swooshes open, and his son Malcolm is there to remind him that the meal is ready and his presence would be appreciated.

"I'll be out in a minute," he smiles, and indeed after a minute he rises, rinses, and steps into the ante room to dry and dress. "The great thing about the sauna," he says as he pulls on a t-shirt, "is that it cleans you from the inside out."

And having divested himself of that resonant chop, he emerges, clean, into the afternoon sun.

The Siderno of the North

Of the hundred-odd magazine features that I have written over the past twenty years, this is the only one that began with the outright theft of an idea. The woman I robbed, Annette O'Brien (a willing victim and accomplice, I might add), had written a good piece about Schreiber for, I think, *Lake Superior* magazine, and had shown it to me at a writers' workshop I led in Thunder Bay in 1991. I was impressed immediately by the notion of a Canadian village of Italians, most of them related to one another and almost all descended from the same smallish city in southern Italy. I asked Annette if she'd mind if I, too, did a piece on Schreiber, and she was discreet enough to say she didn't. So I did.

As it turned out, my discomfort over this journalistic trespass—less a crime than a sin—lingered to the point that, every time I saw Annette during the two or three years that followed the publication of the story, I felt obliged to grovel up to her and beg her pardon once again for my pathetic scruples and lack of imagination in working out my own ideas. I'd probably be grovelling still, except that, one day, she fixed me with a squint and said, "Would you please stop apologizing about Schreiber! I don't care! I was happy to give you the idea!"

For me, the legacy of the story has been a brace of friendships and acquaintances that give my family and me reason to stop in Schreiber every time we go through. During the past few years, we have enjoyed the hospitality of Teresa Stortini, Schreiber's recently retired librarian; and of Peter and Tina Speziale at the Sunset Motel. I have followed with fascination the international boxing career of Dominic Filane; and have dozens of times been on the receiving end of Pina Commisso's culinary skill and generosity at Rosie and Josie's Restaurant. During the couple of years after the story appeared, Pina stubbornly refused payment for even the most lavish meals that my family and I consumed in the restaurant. I recall with nostalgia that our first meal in Thunder Bay, in the autumn of 1991, was three immense home-made panzarottis that Pina had given us the night before, during a meal stop on the anchor leg of our drive to Thunder Bay.

Many things have changed in Schreiber since I wrote: the railway has laid off dozens of mechanics, brakemen and yard men; Rollie Stortini, a considerate, intelligent man, who I interviewed in preparing the article, has passed on; his wife Teresa has retired from the library. After fifty-two years on the job, Peter Speziale, who figures prominantly in the article, has retired as manager of Spadoni's Department Store. And Rosa Diano (the "Rosie" in "Rosie and Josie's") has left the restaurant business. A year or two ago, boxer Dominic Filane returned to town, as he told me he might during my research for the article. In the space above the family gas bar and store, where he once pounded the speed bag in preparation for the Olympics, he now runs a fledgling sportswear and cresting business.

I am entirely innocent about the protocol for dedicating particular sections of a book to particular people. But notwithstanding the general dedication on the book's second leaf, I feel I should commit the next eight or nine pages to Annette O'Brien, without whom this particular version of the story of Schreiber would not exist. For Annette, then, with final apologies.

THE AFTERNOON SKY is a dense mass of gun-metal clouds, and an unfriendly breeze sweeps up from Lake Superior, swirling through the streets of Schreiber, Ontario. It is late July, and in contrast to the weather outside, the wedding at Holy Angels Church glows all the brighter. It is a radiant affair, a showpiece: three flower girls (one of whom distributes a chrysanthemum to every female guest), two ring bearers, six bridesmaids, six ushers. The altar is laden with gladioluses and mums, and a clump of baby's breath marks every pew.

As the glittering procession inches up the aisle, as the video cameras whir (there are four of them in operation), a glacial soprano voice soars from the balcony behind:

We're on our way to say "I do."
Our secret dreams have all come true.

Finally comes the bride, the home-town beauty, solemn and luminous, festooned for the day in silk and jewellery. Raise high the roofbeams—seldom has a wedding shone with more lustre.

As the new Mr. and Mrs. Gisella and Giullio Lalli emerge from the church, the crowd of guests spills out onto the lawn. They weep and embrace and kiss. Without exception, they are dark-eyed and dark-complexioned. A few of the elder guests might have stepped directly from the villages and fields of their ancestral homeland in the Calabria region of Italy.

Eventually, the celebrants pile into decorated cars and parade through town, honking and hamming. To get added mileage out of the revels (there are just 10 kilometres of road in Schreiber) they are obliged to make two or three passes along the main street. "Here they come again!" squeals a delighted youngster.

At the reception that night, there are perhaps 350 in attendance, many more than at the ceremony. The dinner is a textbook of Italian cuisine: antipasto, prosciutto, manicotti, penne, scampi, veal parmigiana, gellato...and, of course, barrels of red and white wine, most of the bottles carefully stripped of their labels and reincarnated as vintage "Gisella & Giullio."

With dinner done, the party begins in earnest: jiving, waltzing, Italian folk dancing, and, at the high point of the evening, the Italian Tarantella dance, a frenetic outpouring of emotion and energy choreographed centuries ago to suggest the effects of the tarantula spider's calamitous bite. At one point in the strenuous ritual, a thick-set carouser staggers from the dance floor, the back of his suit coat ripped from collar to belt line.

As the party ebbs and flows, family members are rounded up in groups and shunted off for photo sessions. "Say *formaggio!*" cries the photographer, and the gang hollers out the word.

On the face of things, there is nothing exceptional about the town of Schreiber on the north shore of Lake Superior, some 200 kilometres east of Thunder Bay. Its economy runs on railroading, mining, forest products, and on serving the endless stream of truckers and tourists who motor through on the Trans-Canada Highway. The town supports four churches, several stores and restaurants, two schools, a handful of motels and garages, a train station, and that fixture of small-town life in Canada, a hockey arena.

A glance at the phone book, however, reveals a disproportionate presence of tongue-tripping Italian surnames: 13 Figliomenis, 13 Commissos, 12 Speziales, 13 Costas, and a host of Caccamos, Cebrarios, Dianos, Pellegrinos, Spadonis, and so on down to the Valentinos, Venezianos and Verdones.

The town, it would seem, might better have been named for an Italian patriarch or poet than for the 19th-century English engineer and CPR builder, Sir Collingwood Schreiber. Fully half of its population of 2,000 is of Italian descent. Moreover, almost all the town's Italian inhabitants are related. "It didn't start out that way," laughs Schreiber resident Cosimo Filane. "But over the years, somebody from one family would marry somebody from another, and so on, to the point where almost everyone was connected to almost everyone else—at least by marriage."

So extensive are the family connections—and the resulting duplication of names—that many of the men in Schreiber's Italian community are more commonly identified by the names of their businesses than by their birth names. Cousins Peter and Peter Speziale are known best as Western Pete and Spadoni Pete (for their respective management of the local Western Tire store and of Spadoni's Department Store). Jimmy Speziale owns the Shell station—hence Jimmy Shell. Garage owners Joe Figliomeni and Cosimo Figliomeni are better known as Texaco Joe and Texaco Coe ("Joe Tex and Coe Tex would have been simpler," cracks a local business owner, "but we have to keep things respectable.").

Some of the town's Italians work on the railroad or in the Kimberly-Clark pulp mill at nearby Terrace Bay, but the largest portion by far works in local commerce. Italian names predominate in Schreiber's business community: Costa's Supermarket, Cebrario's Hardware & Lumber, Spadoni Brothers GM dealership, Figliomeni's Trailer Park, the Cosiana Inn, the Villa Bianca Inn & Restaurant, Filane's Fallen Rock Motel, Speziale's Sunset Motel.

Pina Commisso is the dedicated owner of Rosie and Josie's Restaurant, where twice a week she cooks up 300-litre lots of tomato sauce and prepares 100-kilo batches of fresh pasta for the enjoyment of travellers and truckers. "It doesn't matter whether I'm heading east or west, I always hang on until Schreiber, to load up at Rosie and Josie's," says Vancouver transport driver Martin Crew, who drives a regular trans-Canada route.

On the wall at Rosie and Josie's there is a framed colour photo of a pair of ice-covered Via Rail diesels, trans-continentals, sitting nose to nose in the local station. "Frozen up, Feb. 8, 1989," reads a small metal plate attached to the frame. Nearby hangs an aerial photo of the picturesque city of Siderno Marina, spread out between the arid mountains and the wide brown beaches of the Ionian Sea in southern Italy.

The only visible link between the photos is that, in each, a range of ancient mountains nestles up to the edges of civilization.

Pina Commisso, owner, manager and chef at Rosie and Josie's Italian restaurant, on the Trans-Canada Highway.

But there is a deeper connection that nourishes the genealogy of nearly every Italian in Schreiber: Fully 95 per cent of the town's Italian population have their roots in the tidy red-roofed city depicted in the photo. "It's a phenomenon!" exclaims one Schreiber resident. "It's as if a few hardy seeds from Siderno had been brought here, planted, and had flourished in this little northern garden. You'd think no one from a sweltering southern climate could even survive here, let alone prosper."

The first of Siderno's male expatriates arrived in the Schreiber area, without their families, during the late 1800s. They had been lured by the promise of jobs in the forests or in the construction of the Canadian Pacific Railway. In contrast to Siderno, where most men and women tended hillside gardens and orchards for wealthy *padrones*, Canada offered not just a chance to make a living wage, but the rarer possibility of land ownership.

"My grandfather came over and worked on the railway, while my grandmother raised the family back home," says Peter Speziale, his English inflected by a melodious Italian lilt. "Grandpa made a bit of a stake, and when my daddy was old enough, he came to Schreiber because his father was here." Peter himself arrived as a teenager in 1939 to join his father and a growing aggregation of Figliomenis, Costas, Commissos and Spadonis, all of whom had long since accepted cultural uprooting and fierce northern winters as the price of opportunity. Even those who did not prosper immediately were no worse off than they had been in Calabria, one of the poorest and least fertile regions of Italy.

While Italian settlement in the Schreiber area proceeded smoothly through the early decades of the century, the late 1930s and early 1940s were not banner years for Italian immigrants. Because Italy's dictator Benito Mussolini supported Adolf Hitler, Italians in Canada were considered potential collaborators with the fascists and possible saboteurs of the Canadian war effort. Some immigrants were rounded up and placed in internment camps, while others, such as Peter Speziale, were obliged to report regularly to the authorities on their whereabouts and activities. Speziale believes that most of the Italians in the Schreiber area— and, indeed, throughout the country—had little interest in the fascists back home, and that those *with* an interest were almost certainly as contemptuous of them as were most Canadians. "Of course as the war passed," he says, "things gradually returned to normal, and everything was forgiven." If not as quickly forgotten.

Originally Ojibwa territory, the Schreiber area was first settled by Europeans in 1870, when Colonel James Isbester and his troops came ashore at present day Schreiber Beach on their way to put down the Riel Rebellion in western Canada. The colonel dubbed the spot Isbester's Landing, a name that lasted until the early 1880s, when railway construction became the major local industry and the settlement was renamed Schreiber, in honour of the CPR's chief engineer at the time.

With the completion of the transcontinental railway in 1886, the community became an important CPR divisional point, with engine repair shops, car barns and maintenance equipment. At about the same time, gold and zinc mining began in the area, fluctuating vastly in profitability through much of the 20th century. Today, the local mining industry is represented by just one company, Inmet Inc., which extracts zinc, lead and copper ore from the Williams Lake Mine some fifteen kilometres northwest of town (the mine attracted national attention in April, 1997, when Schreiber resident Terry Fairservice was killed at the site in a cave-in). Railway activity has significantly diminished in Schreiber over the past few years, but the railway is still one of the area's main employers, along with the Kimberly-Clark plant in Terrace Bay and the Williams Lake Mine.

For most of the town's Italians, life has been prosperous in recent years, thanks largely to the community's assiduous work habits. "If Italians had been afraid of hard work, they'd never have survived here in the first place," says Carlo Falcioni, a recent visitor to Schreiber from Sudbury. "When the immigrants came to Montreal at the turn of the century, there would be railway agents with interpreters at the train station to recruit them for jobs, because they knew that you couldn't go wrong with an Italian."

The scions of those early immigrants are still known to put in exhaustingly long work days in their various businesses. Pina Commisso often begins work at Rosie and Josie's as early as 6 a.m.

and does not finish until well after nightfall. Until his recent retirement, Peter Speziale worked long hours as manager of Spadoni's Department Store, then went home to operate the family motel, with his wife, Tina, and son, Dennis, who holds a full-time job with the railway.

One of the town's best known citizens, Cosimo Filane, owns two motels, a variety store, a fast-food restaurant, and a gas station—a small empire which would be impossible to maintain without extensive help from his wife, Diana, and family. Over the years, Filane has also found time to develop a singing career and to cut four record albums, as well as coaching local hockey and writing a novel about the community of "Fallen Rock," a fictional town with an uncanny resemblance to Schreiber. The talented entrepreneur (whose name combines the first two letters of his baptismal name, Figliomeni, with the surname of Frankie Lane, one of his early singing idols) has had the pleasure of seeing his own ambition reborn in his children, two of whom have found fame in the punishing sport of boxing. Son Dominic, a graduate of Seneca College in Toronto and a former Canadian amateur light flyweight champion (to 48 kg.), fought in both the Barcelona and Atlanta Olympic Games. Son Gerry, also a graduate of Seneca College, was at one time Canadian amateur lightweight champion (56-60 kg.). Over the years, the brothers have done extensive training in a make-shift gym above the family's variety store and gas bar, within metres of the Trans-Canada Highway. "My coach tells me we have great bloodlines for the sport," smiles the amiable Dominic, "an Irish mother, an Italian father."

Like the rest of Schreiber's Italians, the Filanes, Speziales and Commissos have happily integrated themselves into the mainstream of Canadian life. But they have done so without relinquishing the distinctive traditions and touchstones that tie them to the old country and sustain their cultural identity. Many of those traditions centre around the family dining table. "At our house, we eat spaghetti every Thursday and every Sunday," says Cosimo Filane. "Almost everybody in Schreiber does. That's the way our parents did it and their parents, too."

Schreiber gardens tend to feature Italian staples such as tomatoes, beans and herbs, and dozens of the town's Italian families make an annual event of winemaking or of the preparation of Italian sausage. "When my husband Rollie was building our house," says former town librarian Teresa Stortini, "the wine cellar was the first room he finished." Until Rollie's death in 1992, the Stortinis (one of few Schreiber families with roots in central and northern Italy) got together with friends every September to

Olympic boxer Dominic Filane, seen here in the tropics, a ways south of Schreiber.

crush sixty to seventy cases of grapes, yielding some 700 litres of wine. "We used to put our share in big open vats in the basement to ferment, then open the windows to let the fumes out," says Teresa. "With everybody in town making their wine at about the same time, you can get quite a fragrance out in the streets."

Once a year, on a Saturday in early November, a group of the most committed winemakers in Schreiber gets together and goes house-to-house tasting one another's product. On the same night, at an anonymous tasting, they choose the best wine of the year and celebrate the vintage with a feast that has taken as long as two days to prepare.

Of all the community's traditions, however, it is the local weddings, with their lavish trappings and codified rituals, that perhaps best represent ancestral links with the old country. "In rare cases you'll still even get an arranged marriage in Schreiber," says Teresa Stortini. "Beyond that, there's certainly still a fair bit of parental pressure as to who a kid *should* marry. It's one way of keeping the Italian community strong." Suddenly, she is laughing: "I can't say I'd want to try to tell my own kids who they should or shouldn't marry."

Like weddings back home, those in Schreiber can bring together as many as five hundred guests, most of them related. They come from across the continent and, of course, from Italy. If the numbers necessitate it, wedding receptions are held not in the local recreation hall but on the floor of the Schreiber arena. The community's commitment to those sybaritic rites is sufficiently strong that parents cheerfully accept the spending of thousands of dollars—in some cases $20,000 or more—to stage the events. "In this town, it's a tradition you just don't violate," says Cosimo Filane. Although Cosimo and Diana were married in Thunder Bay, they spent their honeymoon in Siderno, in honour of Cosimo's roots.

Considering the size and tradtions of Schreiber's Italian community, it is surprising that there is no emphasis in the local schools on Italian culture or on the history of Italian settlement in Canada. Nor does the curriculum offer any courses in the language. "The Italians aren't at all pushy about their way of life," says one local teacher who requested anonymity. "Probably if they demanded some input into the curriculum, they'd get it—particularly in the separate school, which is crowded with their kids. Then again, there might be resistance from the non-Italian parents."

As it is, Italian is widely spoken in Schreiber homes, although seldom in public. According to Teresa Stortini people feel that "because they're here in Canada, they'll speak the prevailing language."

"The unfortunate thing," says Cosimo Filane, "is that the younger generation doesn't bother with the language at all. I sing a couple of Italian numbers, but I don't speak it much since my father died." Filane believes, nevertheless, that as long as there are Italians in Schreiber, aspects of the culture will survive. "You lose a little in every generation, but in a small town, it's easier to keep it going than it is in a city. You don't have so many influences and distractions to draw people away from it."

Dominic Filane endorses his father's views, while allowing that, for most of the community's young people, the future is not in Schreiber but elsewhere. "I'm not saying that I wouldn't come back here to live some day. I might. When you're raised here, you've got the forest and and lake in your blood just as much as the Italian traditions. It's not an easy place to walk away from."

Dominic acknowledges that when he is away from town for a while, he finds himself longing to get back to friends, family and familiar surroundings. "Then when I'm in Schreiber for a while, I'll be telling myself, 'I've gotta go. I've gotta go.' There just aren't the opportunities here."

A hundred years ago, Dominic's forefathers left Siderno for the same reason people leave Schreiber today: opportunities elsewhere. They came to the north shore of Lake Superior, made a home of the place, and re-established the traditions they had left behind.

"If we've done a good job as parents, our own young people will do the same thing when they go," says a rather wistful Peter Speziale. "Those who stay will survive, too, of course."

"Survival," he adds, "is part of what it is to be Italian."

The Lifelong Smell of Summer

The geographical axis of this brief personal essay is a drunken line running from northern Manitoba southward to Lake of the Woods, east to the Soo, then south again into central Ontario. While parts of the essay focus on the area around Thunder Bay, the heart of the piece lies somewhat further east. Its *spirit*, however, is so entirely transferable to this part of the country that I have no qualms about including it in a collection that purports to be about northwestern Ontario. For one thing it is about woods and lakes and camp life...and of course about summer, a season well loved in a region where, during the average year, winter comes half a dozen times, consuming much of what time the Gregorian calendar traditionally assigns to spring and fall.

Summer, by comparison, is a blown kiss, a dream world, that we are always glad to be reminded will, somehow, come again. I wrote this piece during the snowbound dreariness of February 1997, when I needed such a reminder.

A S A KID, I sucked my thumb vigorously, *reverentially*, at any hour of the day or night. For that reason, I was familiar with a variety of subtle fragrances that I'd never have known otherwise, each brought to my nose from whatever surfaces or substances my left hand had been up against when I opted for a pull on my built-in soother. Better than most I knew the smell of crayons, baseball cards, sand boxes, soil, marsh water, dew worms, comic books, knife and scissor handles, coins, bike tires, the interior of baseball gloves (I caught and sucked left).

Because I occasionally washed my hands, I could distinguish Ivory from Camay from Palmolive—or, at the cottage, Sunlight, which, during the 1950s, my mother used for hand-scrubbing summer laundry (the pearl soft water that I hauled by the bucketload from Clear Lake was good for cottons, skin and hair; bad for tea and coffee).

It gives me limited satisfaction to think my thumbsucking was useful for something other than bucking my front teeth, which it did nicely. But I cannot help speculating that it was also the root of a heightened olfactory sensibility that I might never have possessed had I forsaken my thumb, as most do, by the age of one or two.

I am by no means a sniffer on the order of the hound or ferret. The shortcomings of nose were impressed upon me several summers ago on a day-long fishing trip to Lac des Mille Lacs near Ignace in northwestern Ontario. By mid-afternoon, our little party had a couple of pike, half a dozen pickerel and a rainbow trout on the stringer. Our cooler was empty, and the sun had burned a dreary white hole in our enthusiasm for the day.

Out of his evolving funk, my friend Eric Stoneman said, "Did you know you can identify fish by their smell?"

"Who can?" I said.

"I can."

Within seconds, Eric's 15-year-old son had his hands clamped over his dad's eyes from behind, and I had two-pound trout beneath his nose.

"Trout," he said confidently.

I held up a pickerel, and he said "Pickerel."

Reluctant to believe that anyone's nose could be *that* sensitive, I picked up a chunk of rough-cut two-by-eight, a discarded piece of barn flooring that had been used as a fish-cleaning board throughout the summer and was rank with the juices of at least four species. Eric sniffed at it for several seconds at close range but said nothing.

"So, what is it?" I demanded.

"Hemlock," he said quietly. "It's hard to distinguish from spruce."

The young protagonist in Heinrich Böll's novel, *The Clown*, was so sensitively disposed toward smells that he could identify them over the phone.

What I possess, by comparison, is less an instrument of detection than an *appreciation* of smells, as a key both to the physical world and to such higher imponderables as memory, longing and desire.

Because summer is the time for smells in this climate (statistically, there are thirteen warm-weather smells for every cold-weather smell), and because my deepest understanding of the season evolves from the cottage at Torrance, Ontario, where I have spent at least part of every summer since I was less than a year old, I can, to this day, recreate my summers as a kind of olfactory rubbing of that place, its surroundings, and a lifetime's activities there. My wife, Betty, feels much the same way about summers spent on the lakes and rivers around Lynn Lake and Leaf Rapids in far northern Manitoba. Indeed, on an afternoon last July, on a stretch of the Trans-Canada between Thunder Bay and the Soo, we indulged in a lengthy impromptu recollection of the myriad of smells that, for us, evoked the richness and variety of those places at that time of year: the mosses and pines and spruce trees; fish frying in the cast iron pan; coffee being brewed in the old metal percolator; the rocks and soil of the berry patch and, of course, blueberries, strawberries and raspberries being baked into pies or boiled into jam or preserves.

Betty recalled the interior of tents; popcorn and marshmallows on the open fire; Coleman and kerosene lamps; galvanized pails and washtubs; the way the road or woods or air smelled after a rain.

I mentioned the pine cones that my sisters and I would gather for my mother who used them as kindling for the kitchen stove, and the chunks of green apple she'd occasionally toss onto the stove top to sweeten the air. And how my dad could distinguish fresh-split pine, balsam, and hemlock, as well as the subtler fragrances of maple, birch, poplar and ash. The process of starting the morning fire in the woodstove was a succession of smells, beginning at the woodbox with the organic mustiness of old bark, followed by the surprise assault of a struck wooden match; the flash flame of newsprint and kindling; then the woodsmoke proper, overbearing when it leaked into the cabin or cottage, but as rich an opiate as you could hope for when you stepped outside and caught it adrift on the hint of a morning breeze that had come up out of the west at the far end of the lake (the word perfume comes from the Latin noun *fumus*, meaning smoke).

We recalled the cedar swamp; trampled bracken and jewel-weed; picked mushrooms; funguses knocked from the bark of rotting trees; roadside clover; the seductive whiff of sweetgrass.

The waterfront is not so much a source as a sea of nasal nostalgia: plastic water toys, life jackets, wet bathing suits. We named the dock and the tombs beneath it; pickerel weed and spicebush; and, unique to the waterskier, the adrenaline-inducing stink of outboard exhaust as the skier waits in the water, or on the dock, for take-off.

Fish and fish bait. And tackle boxes.

Somewhere in the backwaters of my cerebellum, I can locate the fragrance of every boat I have ever owned: sailboats, runabouts, punts, the sunburnt cedar and varnish of the old canoe.

Though I have not driven my old '65 Sunbeam Alpine in more than twenty years, I remember to the molecule the lusty, leathery, gearboxy smell of its interior on a hot summer day.

It is worth noting that not all of my recollections are pleasant. To this day, the smell of oil-based paint induces dreary memories of the hours I spent brushing a variety of finishes onto the shutters, window trim, fascia, soffits (a chiropractic memory unto itself) and to what in those days seemed vast tracts of cove siding that formed the shell of our ramified shack on Clear Lake at Torrance. One summer, perhaps 1961, a dripless wonder-coating called Thix Alkyd, a gelatinous mystery mush, appeared briefly on the market and disappeared, but not before its rubbery odour made an indelible impression on me, distinct from any other paint I have ever used.

It is a tribute to forgiveness that my Aunt Leone could not remember that, during the late 1950s, on a trip to the municipal dump at Walker's Point north of Gravenhurst, I accidentally spilled a bottle of (very) sour milk onto the back-seat carpet of her Hillman Minx—or that, for the rest of the summer, trips to Gravenhurst or Port Carling became rigorous exercises in shallow breathing.

I am not alone in believing that, where literature is concerned, smell is the most feebly represented of the senses. This is probably because smells do not translate well into print. Or perhaps simply because people do not think much about them. When I began gathering thoughts toward this reminiscence, it occurred to me to discover the degree to which people *did* think about them—or, alternatively, the degree to which I am alone in attaching significance to odours and their evocations. So I asked friends and relatives what smells *they* most associated with summer.

My father, a productive source on almost any subject, offered a variety of of fragrances, including smoke from the railway fires of his boyhood, coal oil lamps, mice and skunks. He also recalled his grandmother's morning "pikelets," little dollops of dough that she would fry up for breakfast at the MacBain family cottage on Clear Lake. He expressly urged me to keep my essay clear of outhouses, particularly (I assume) our own. But to do so would be to pull a punch with no compelling reason to do so—except his urgings. *Our* backhouse smelled less like a backhouse than a mildly musty shed. In fact, it was a merciful little place, an antiquarian repository of obscure novels and old magazines and newspapers. And because it faced the woods and swamp, rather than the cottage or lake, you could leave the door open while you were in there and gaze out at the hemlocks and pines, contemplating the goodness of nature.

My cottage neighbour, George Syme, recalled the heady fragrance of white clover and the paradoxically sweet smell of manure on the fields north of Toronto. His wife Dale named the white pines that are practically an icon in the cottage areas of eastern Canada. My one-time editor, Ann Gander, mentioned the surpassing odour of frying bacon and eggs, in her case an indulgence exclusive to the cottage.

Our (well-painted) cottage burned to the ground in 1976, and, to this day, when I'm under the new cottage I come across remnant pockets of cinders, carrying the stench of terror and loss from that memorably hot day more than two decades ago. It is a curious twist of fate that the musty smell of opening up the new place in early summer has become for me indistinguishable from the smell of opening up the old place. I could speculate that some psychic defence mechanism has kicked in to protect my memories of what was; but the simpler and more plausible explanation is that my sensory acuity—my memory, period—has begun to fade. Like Dylan Thomas, I can seldom remember whether the storm lasted for six days and six nights when I was twelve, or twelve days and twelve nights when I was six.

On the other hand, some inner response that is triggered for me by the flight paths of the senses grows stronger as the years pass. If I shut my eyes, I can summon the oiled floorboards and yeast-heavy air of Don's Bakery in Bala; the organic tanginess of Ing's or Burgess's grocery stores (quite unlike the sweeter air of Hait's or Tonge's grocery stores in Torrance).

I shut my eyes again, and it's gas tanks and suntan oil on the dock; snapping turtles dank with foreboding; steaks and hamburgers on the barbecue.

Departed relatives and neighbours appear: Mrs. McPhail with a platter of hot dogs ("red hots" she called them) for the kids; Grandpa Scholey at his grindstone with its odour of hot metal and minerals; my mother sipping coffee on the swingchairs by the lake, or poised at her easel (now with the coffee beside her on a table).

And thus the summers reconvene, in smells that connect me most deeply to the planet and to myself.

When I asked my fellow writer Jake MacDonald about memorable fragrances, he described what he called "the great, tepid, almost erotic vapour—ozone and algae and so on—that begins to rise off the lake when the water reaches a certain temperature at the end of June or beginning of July. You'll get up some morning to go fishing, or be out in your boat some night, and suddenly there it is, an overwhelming olfactory experience—the true beginning of summer."

There is only one season in men's hearts, said Thoreau.

And in their noses, too.

At whatever time of year that season might happen to come to life.

The Catch

Like the chapter that precedes it, this brief history of fishing as practised by the Wilkins family is a northwestern Ontario story more by subject than by setting. It does touch on Lake of the Woods, but its geographical centre lies far to the east and south, in the piney tourist lands of central Ontario. Understandably, not all stories about fishing in central Ontario echo the fishing that is done in The Great Northwest (as our region has been modestly dubbed by local CBC Radio). This one manages to do so largely because it is not about fishing so much as *un*fishing, virtual fishing, which can be practised as ineptly in this part of the country as in the most crowded resort areas of Muskoka or the Kawarthas. My one small regret about reprinting the piece, which appeared in *Cottage Life* during the summer of 1995, is that we cannot also reproduce Joe Salina's accompanying illustration, a striking piece of work that shows a fat sunfish rising radiantly over the treeline, beaming light onto a father and son as they fish from the end of a dock. You'll have to imagine it.

W HEN THEY WENT into the frying pan—gutted, headless, and scaled—they were shaped like South America. By the time they came out, foreshortened by the heat, they had become Africa and had all the visual appeal of Saharan camel chips.

Nevertheless, if you were willing to put in an effort, you could get up to a tablespoon of bluish-white flesh off their teentsy flanks. And we devoured them with gusto—five, six, seven at a sitting.

Until I was ten or eleven, I had never tasted a freshwater fish other than the tiny sunfish that we harvested by the dozens within twenty or thirty metres of the cottage dock at Torrance, Ontario. Several times a summer we'd hook catfish that would be eaten by my mother. But our hope of catching something sportier was as futile, to use Margaret Atwood's phrase, as "enticing whales with a bent pin."

Of all the anglers I have known, met, or observed, we, the Wilkinses, have the lowest standards, the faintest expectations and the slimmest expertise. And perhaps, needless to say, the least to show for nearly forty years of cheerfully feckless angling.

The pip of our tackle box is neither a galloping Rapala nor a monster Mepps but a spool of cheap nylon line given to me and signed by Rocket Richard, who used to be in the tackle business and about whom I once wrote a chapter in a book. On two occasions that I can think of, more sophisticated fishermen have glimpsed our equipment, a rueful muddle of busted rods and seized reels, and have, out of pity, given us "better" rods and reels that were so complicated we quickly forgot how to use them.

Like my father before me, I have never caught anything on a lure. Nor have my children. Our preferred bait is half an earthworm, or sometimes a leech or crayfish. I once bought frogs at Purk's Place in Bala, Ontario. When I asked Purk how to put them on the hook, he said, "through the lips." I exchanged them for worms.

I have no qualms about admitting that no Wilkins has ever caught his or her limit—or even approched it. In fact, we hardly ever catch a species for which a limit exists. But if we are unknown to the warden, we are by no means strangers to the Fatal Shaman of the Fisheries. Or to the notion of a circumscribed catch. It's just that, unlike most fishermen, our limit has been established not by the judicious souls at the Ministry of Natural Resources but by some hazier, less temporal conclave that, for reasons unknown, has set that limit at MAX ONE, at least where any sport fish is concerned. No Wilkins that I know of has ever been granted even the briefest of dispensations.

We have, on occasion, put our mystic restriction to a respectable test. I once caught a ten-pound carp in the shipping channel of the St. Lawrence River near Lancaster, Ontario. In 1977, my dad caught a miraculous 21-inch bass in front of the cottage. As evidence that a Wilkins had caught such a gargantua, he suggested to my mother that she trace it for posterity. Since she had already cleaned it, she traced it sans head and tail, and

The author with son, Matt (right) and Blake Boddy at Echo Lake.

inscribed the tracing: "Caught by Hume, July 27, 1977, at dusk, on half a rubber worm." As if to dispel any notion that headless smallmouths might be living in Clear Lake, she added the word "cleaned" at the bottom.

She hung the tracing on the wall, where, over the years, it has been joined by a dozen or more such tracings, mostly on cereal-box cardboard (the gallery is nothing if not entirely befitting the spirit of our angling). The smallest of these cutouts depicts a 5-inch rock bass, the first fish caught by my son Matt, in 1992. Another recalls a 9-inch sunfish, and yet another (on purple construction paper) a gloriously tubby smallmouth landed by my nephew John.

Yet another is of a 14-inch catfish, caught in 1980 by my dad. During the fourteen years that followed that particular catch, not one of us caught or saw another catfish, and we grew to believe that the species was gone from the lake. We stopped catching sunfish, too. Rock bass took their place. For several years, I myself was gone from the lake—at least as a fisherman.

Another mighty harvest for Charlie and Matt—Clear Lake, 1993.

Three summers ago, Matthew (then four years old) began working on me to take him fishing. We unravelled some of the same derelict tackle that I had used as a kid, and that my father had used. In August of last year, Matt caught a 14-inch catfish, an anachronism hearkening not just to 1980 but to the years when we caught four or five a summer. A week after that he caught a sunfish, the first in years. He didn't know what it was.

I have sometimes wondered whether the Wilkinses, with our trifling catches and crummy tackle, bear some ancient ichtyological curse. At other times I have wondered whether it is perhaps those guys with $25,000 bass boats and computerized fish finders who are cursed. I once went fishing with such a guy, and he spent most of the morning fiddling anxiously with his fish finder. When he wasn't doing that, he was racing across Lake of the Woods to where he hoped the non-action would be a little less non.

I once said to my father, a man whose indifference to good tackle and technique has been honed to an art form, "What do you think about while you're fishing?"

He said, "fishing."

Last summer while I was out on Clear Lake drowning worms with Matt, I asked him the same question. He said, "getting home and playing video games. What do you think about?"

I pondered for a moment and said, "I think about stuff that's way too hard to explain." Which at that point was as close to the truth as I could get.

The Bikers of the Bird World

Taped to the window in front of my desk, there is a life-sized cardboard cut-out of a raven. Beyond it, I can see what many Thunder Bay residents would consider a typical view of the city, including old forest, ancient mountains and, depending on the time of year, either frozen or open lake. Off and on throughout the day, I can also see real ravens, sitting on wires or rooftops, or in trees…or, occasionally, cruising right up to the eaves on the front verandah, just a few feet from the cardboard raven that I suspect attracts them.

My interest in the corvids—a genus that includes ravens, crows, magpies, blue jays and whisky jacks—began during the late 1970s when I raised a crow near the village of Inwood in the Manitoba Interlake. It expanded greatly when I moved from southern Ontario to Thunder Bay in 1991 and was introduced to the species that my friend Scot Kyle , for reasons that will be explained, occasionally refers to as "the bikers of the bird world."

During the years that have elapsed since, my appreciation of these exceptional creatures—of their athleticism and ingenuity and ability to communicate—has done nothing but expand. Not long ago, on a little spur of railway track near the United Grain Growers elevator south of Marina Park here in Thunder Bay I came across a lone raven hauling a grisly-looking leg of moose, of perhaps a dozen kilos, along the track bed, manipulating one end of it forward, then leaping to the other end and laboriously swinging it round, using the track as a kind of fulcrum, seeming to understand perfectly the mechanical advantage of the first-class lever.

I walked closer, eventually getting down on my haunches and easing up to within a few feet of the bird as it continued to work. When I was almost close enough to touch it, it stopped momentarily, jumped onto its prize and issued a sharp crawk, clearly intended to warn me that I had come close enough. It returned to work and I continued to inch toward it, until again it jumped on the leg, this time gathering itself into a tight bullet of feathers, then exploding out of its compression, loosing a shriek that was so loud, so demented, that in my surprise I lost my balance and half tumbled backward, while the bird, satisfied that it had made the intended impression and determined not to lose what it had gained, jumped forward onto the ground and stood scolding me in a quiet outpouring of invective that did not stop until I had gotten to my feet and backed off.

Since 1994, when the following piece appeared in *Canadian Geographic*, I have had dozens of people contact me, either in person or by letter, to tell me their own raven stories. Because ravens tend to insinuate themselves into human society (and to a lesser degree vice versa), some of these tales sound more like descriptions of old friendships than mere bird anecdotes. Others are barely credible—except perhaps to those who know the ways of the raven. Many of the best of them are included on the pages that follow.

ONE MORNING in November of 1992, Diane Garrick heard a commotion outside her home in the north end of Thunder Bay, Ontario. She went to the window and saw the family border collie scolding a raven that was croaking and fluttering along the eaves of the backyard garage, above the dog's food dish. The bird lured the dog to the far end of the garage, then across the yard to the back fence, where it danced and nagged for two or three minutes, just beyond the dog's reach.

In the meantime, a second raven had swooped down from the rooftop and was devouring the dog's abandoned food. "It was really something," says Garrick, "these two birds working together, completely outwitting this relatively intelligent mammal."

When the second raven had finished eating, it took over the diversionary tactics while the first one flew briefly out of sight before appearing at the dog dish for a meal of its own.

Two years ago, in another Thunder Bay neighbourhood, biologist Ted Armstrong put several pieces of "very dry, hard bread" on the bird feeder outside his home. "Sometime later, my wife and I saw a raven eating a piece of this bread out of the nearby bird-bath," he says. Armstrong's first thought was that the bread had fallen from the feeder and somehow landed in the bath. "When it happened again, we realized that the raven was taking the bread and soaking it to soften it up—in effect making porridge," says Armstrong.

Whoever coined the term "birdbrain" as a synonym for dunce or simpleton could not have known much about the capabilities of the common raven. This large black bird, *Corvus corax*, is common in name and occurrence only. In most aspects of its storied existence, it is decidedly uncommon. Evidence of its extraordinary intelligence is both anecdotal and scientific. Laboratory tests conducted during the 1950s by German zoologist Otto Kohler showed, for example, that ravens are able to distinguish numbers and, in effect, to count. Field observations have shown that the bird has at least seven distinct calls and can imitate the calls of other birds. Some ravens even possess what could only be described as a sense of humour. A recent CBC Radio report from Yellowknife described how ravens in that city have been known to perch on the sloped metal roofs of commercial buildings, waiting for people to pass below. At the opportune moment, for no apparent reason other than mischief, the birds loosen the accumulated snow, sending it careening down the slippery metal onto unsuspecting pedestrians.

"There are a number of 'smart' birds out there," says Thunder Bay biologist Tom Baxter, a former naturalist at Lake Superior Provincial Park, "but it would be difficult to name one with the combined mental *and* physical capacities of the raven. It's an athletic bird, it's hardy, it's adaptable, and all in very high measure."

The very "commonness" of the raven's occurrence is exceptional. "Its breeding grounds cover most of the land mass of the northern hemisphere, right around the globe," say ornithologist John Ryder of Lakehead University. "Very few birds are anywhere near that widely spread."

In keeping with its impressive range and capabilities, the raven's place in world literature and folklore is both extensive and varied, dating back through 4,000 years of recorded or spoken history. It is well noted in writings that range from the Bible and Norse legends to the works of Shakespeare, Dante and Edgar Allan Poe. It features prominently in novels as diverse as Dickens' *Barnaby Rudge* and Mordecai Richler's *Solomon Gursky Was Here*. It is a mainstay of the ancient legends of Europe, the Orient and the Middle East, and is extensively mythlogized by the Haida of Canada's West Coast, who call the bird the "Trickster."

The bird's savvy is a function of its highly evolved brain. "The hyperstratium, the part of the brain responsible for learning and intelligence in birds, is very much enlarged in this species," says Ryder. He compares the hyperstriatum to the human cerebral cortex, and notes that the size of the organ is responsible for the raven's "tremendous success" in exploiting its environment. "The bird is a real opportunist," he says, "particularly in its close relationship with human beings." One of the axioms of the North, in fact, is that where there are people, there are ravens. "They tend to stay pretty much on their own during summer when the food supply is good in the wilds. But come fall, they converge on the towns and settlements, where they go after almost anything edible that people throw out or leave behind," says Ryder.

In their obsessive scavenging, the birds have been known to keep watch on hunters or fishermen for days, waiting for the butchered or filleted carcasses that will eventually be left. They cruise landfill sites, patrol the streets on garbage day, and ransack dumpsters outside restaurants. They monitor the highways for road kill.

"A successful raven learns very young what a highway is," says Baxter. "They're usually the first on the scene when an animal gets hit by a car, and they can be ruthless in protecting their find." Even the ingenious fox is a poor match for the raven in competition for roadside meals. "I've heard of situations where a raven will descend on a feeding fox, pecking its head and eyes, simply harassing it, until it takes off," says Baxter.

"Ravens are the bikers of the bird world," says Scot Kyle of Thunder Bay. "They're big, they're black, and they're mean." Perhaps predictably, the birds' opportunistic tendencies do not always serve their best interests. During the early 20th century in southern Ontario, for example, they were considered such a threat to crops and young farm animals—they were said to peck the eyes out of calves and lambs, and to kill them—that they were entirely driven out of that part of the country. In recent years, there have been documented reports of ravens killing young cattle in Dryden, Ontario, and The Pas, Manitoba. According to John Ryder, however, their reputation for such behaviour is far larger than their actual aptitude for it. "They tend to be scavengers more than predators," he says.

Ravens have successfully repopulated central and southern Ontario, largely because of the proliferation of landfill sites near towns and cities. "These days," says Ryder, "they can more or less stay out of the farmers' way and still thrive."

Even in nesting, ravens have found ways to capitalize on their affinity for human settlement. Normally they nest on cliffs and in trees, or on the ground in the far north. But they have also been known to nest under highway bridges, in the walls of open pit mines and, in one case in Sudbury, in a satellite dish. For several years during the early 1990s, a pair nested at the top of a 40-metre steel hydro tower on Junot Avenue in Thunder Bay.

Ravens' nests are built of elaborately interwoven sticks, and are generally about 70 to 75 centimetres in diameter and up to 70 centimetres deep. The birds line their nests with the hair of deer, moose, caribou, sheep, skunks, foxes, bobcats—virtually any animal hair they can scavenge from carcasses. Nests built in or near human settlements frequently contain shredded rope, fabric or upholstery stuffing. In 1993, Vancouver naturalist Norah Adkins discovered a nest lined with neatly torn strips of what had obviously been a felt fedora hat. Ravens have been known to use the same nesting site for a hundred years or more, often simply patching up the nest of a previous generation, or incorporating an existing nest into a new structure. "I've seen nests that have been rebuilt so many times," says Adkins, "they end up weighing three or four hundred pounds."

Ravens lay four or five eggs on average, increasing their chances of survival by breeding as early as February when there is less competition for food from other birds. "You'd think when the eggs hatch in late March or April, the nestlings would have a rough time of it," says Ted Armstrong. "But they're pretty tough even at that stage. And because the weather hasn't warmed up yet, many birds and mammals are still in a time of high mortality, so food in the form of carrion is plentiful."

The "tough" nestling eventually becomes one of the hardiest creatures in the animal kingdom. "We used to get blizzards in Wawa (Ontario) when the temperature with the windchill would be fifty below, snow blowing everywhere, and you'd peer out the window through the gusts and see ravens soaring around as if nothing was going on!" says Tom Baxter. "Every once in a while one of them would drop down and go poking into the drifts, digging at a garbage bag that had been left for pick-up. These birds *thrive* in temperatures that almost no other bird or animal can even tolerate."

The raven's diet—a vast, sometimes filthy, smorgasbord—is in itself a measure of the bird's hardiness. During severe winters in the far north, when very little food is available, ravens will follow dog teams and fight for the dogs' steaming dung. They are inveterate thieves of the eggs and young of other birds and, like gulls, will occasionally follow a plow for the worms and insects it turns up. Depending on locale, the typical raven menu can include carrion of every kind (in state of freshness or decay), maggots, mice, rats, lizards, snakes, frogs, crayfish, tadpoles, minnows, the bait from traps, marine invertebrates and molluscs, seeds and berries of many kinds, the buds of trees when food is scarce—and, of course, garbage. "Until the white man came along, ravens on this continent didn't know anything about garbage," says John Ryder. "The aboriginal tribes didn't leave anything of interest to ravens. Now it would seem that the birds consider human beings a visual clue that garbage can't be far off, and they're quick to teach their young that human beings equal relatively easy food."

Exactly how ravens impart this sort of knowledge to their young is not fully understood. "It's often a matter of example, certainly," says Baxter. But as ravens get older, their communications with one another get more subtle, depending increasingly on a complex application of vocalizations. Beyond their most recognizable croak (a lower-pitched, throatier call than the "caw" of the crow), their "language" includes a popping sound like that of cork being pulled from a bottle; a sound often described as a bell-like *croank croank*; and a quiet *thrung, thrung, thrung,* similar to the twang of a tuning fork. Their *gro, gro, gro* sound is generally associated with the exchange of food between parents and young, while the softer crawk and a kind of chuckle are used during mating and incubation.

Ravens also employ an array of more obscure vocalizations that include a sepulchral laugh, *haw-haw-haw,* buzzing and gurgling sounds, and a drawn-out warble, generally heard as a kind of conversation among a number of birds at roost. "It's a measure of their intelligence," says Baxter, "that they can also imitate the calls of other birds—at least those in their voice range. There doesn't seem to be a satisfactory explanation as to why they do this, but you'll hear something that sounds like a goose or jay or especially a crow—they do a great crow impression—and you'll look up and realize it's a raven."

Even in appearance, ravens are frequently confused with crows, particularly at a distance or in flight, when their significantly larger size cannot be used as a means of comparison. "One identifying difference in flight," says John Ryder, "is that the tip of the raven's tail is wedge-shaped—it comes to a shallow point—while the crow's is more or less flat across the tip. But you have to be pretty well right underneath them to see that."

"For me, the significant difference other than the call is that ravens soar, crows don't," says Scot Kyle. "You'll see a raven catch an updraft by a cliff and ride it for three or four minutes, looking around for food. Crows *glide* some when they're coming in for a landing, for instance, but they never soar."

The raven is occasionally referred to as the "black hawk" because of its soaring capability, but its truest distinction as a flyer comes from its aerobatics. "You'll see a raven rise on an updraft," says Baxter, "then fold its wings and drop like a bomb, head first, fifteen, twenty metres, then suddenly spread its wings again and tumble head over tail before levelling out." Ravens have been known to somersault two or three times in succession, and are capable of rolling laterally—"barrel-rolling" as it is sometimes called—or even flying briefly upside down. "For the most part, this sort of stunt flying is part of their mating display," Baxter explains, "but at times it may well be done just for the fun of it."

It has long been assumed that ravens and crows could not interbreed. The species were thought to hate one another so much that even testing the possibility was never attempted. But in recent years, a lone raven living in Metro Toronto—well south of typical raven range—has had a crow as its sole partner. In the spring of 1991, birdwatcher Beth Jefferson saw the male raven copulating with the crow on a lawn in Toronto's west end. Sometime afterward, the crow began sitting on a nest in a spruce tree, while the raven stood guard or brought food to its mate. Then in mid-June, the crow and raven were seen near the nest with two fledglings, presumed to be the offspring of the raven and crow.

If the viability of long-term relations between ravens and crows is to be questioned, it might well be in the light of the ravens' significantly superior intelligence. In an experiment conducted by zoology professor Bernd Heinrich at the University of Vermont, pieces of fresh meat were suspended on three-foot strings from perches in the enclosures of a captive raven and crow. By using both its beak and foot to haul the string in, and raise the meat to the perch, the raven got to it within hours. The crow had not solved the problem after thirty days.

Despite its exceptional habits and intelligence, "the raven is not respected as much as it should be," says John Ryder. "It's been persecuted by white men, largely, I imagine, because of its occasional attacks on farm animals." In various parts of North America, bounties have at times been offered for ravens. Ryder notes that, on the whole, the raven has probably done farmers "more good than harm" by consuming vast numbers of insects, cutworms and vermin.

"Birdwatchers are much more aware—and more respectful—of the raven's special qualities," says Ryder. "The raven is the territorial bird of the Northwest Territories, and it wouldn't be if it wasn't very highly thought of. It's certainly well respected by the aboriginals."

During the 1930s, American biologist Herber Friedman excavated thousands of bones of some forty-five large bird species on

St. Lawrence Island near the Bering Strait. The bones had been buried in pits during a period of more than 2,200 years, and represented the total number of species killed for food or feathers by the natives of the area during that time. "The absence of raven bones," writes American naturalist Henry Collins, in *Birds In Our Lives* , "shows that in prehistoric times, just as today, the raven was regarded as sacred (by the Inuit) and was never killed."

"So you get views of ravens that range from sacred symbol to pest to biological curiosity," says Baxter. "But no matter what our view of them, they seem to be attracted to us. It's a rather complex relationship."

Which is perhaps to be expected of two rather complex species.

What follows appeared as a sidebar to the preceding story. It is a condensation of my own knowledge of ravens, and of material grazed from Shakespeare, the Bible, and half a dozen books on legend, mythology and bird life.

THE TRICKSTER

The complexity of the raven's life in nature is richly mirrored by its diverse place in folklore and literature. Over the centuries, the bird has been portrayed by storytellers and writers as both a benevolent and an evil presence, a sign of hope and an omen of disaster. The ambivalence goes back at least as far as the recording of the Old Testament, some 2,000 years before the birth of Christ. In Genesis, chapter 7, for instance, Noah is said to have released a raven and a dove from the Ark. There is scholarly suggestion that the raven's subsequent abandonment of the Ark, and the dove's hopeful return, may have led to their early reputations as respective agents of despair and hope. In Isaiah 34, the bird is portrayed as a symbol of desolation and, in the Book of Leviticus, is ruled out as a bird worthy of sacrifice to God.

As early as the Old Testament Books of the Kings, however, an opposing, parallel view of the raven emerges. When the prophet Elijah antagonizes King Ahab and Queen Jezebel by foretelling a

The raven—known among the Haida as "the Trickster."

drought in Israel (1 Kings 17), God directs him into hiding, promising that ravens will feed him. "And the ravens brought him bread and meat in the morning, and bread and meat in the evening." Elsewhere in the Bible—Job 38, Psalm 147, Luke 7—God is reported to have provided food for ravens.

Shakespeare's ravens appear as images of the doomed armies in *Julius Caesar* and *King John*, and croak "the fatal entrance of Duncan" in *Macbeth*. In *A Winter's Tale* and *Titus Andronicus*, however, the birds are depicted as benefactors—nurses, if you will—to a "poor babe" and to "forlorn children."

Charles Dickens cast the raven as a figure of amusement in his novel *Barnaby Rudge*. Reviewing the book for a Philadelphia newspaper in 1841, Edgar Allan Poe reproached the famous novelist for failing to realize the raven's "full potential" as an embodiment of gloom. Poe subsequently penned his well-known poem "The Raven," in which the bird, as school children once learned, appears as an agent of lovelessness and despair.

In many parts of Europe, Asia and Africa, the croaking raven is thought to portend death, while in Siberia and parts of aboriginal

North America it signifies life and creation. In yet other cultures, the bird has been imbued with a kind of talismanic potency. Ancient Czecho-Slovak teachings suggest that a hunter who eats the hearts of three ravens reduced to ashes will become an expert shot. Welsh legend implies that blind people who are kind to ravens will regain their sight. Both notions are apparently related to the raven's tendency to attack the eyes of its intended prey or to eat the eyes of a carcass (the tenderest morsels) before other parts. The ancients believed that, having eaten the eyes of its victims, the raven acquired their cumulative sight—an advantage that could be passed on to those who, in turn, ate or even touched the bird.

Irish folklore portrays the raven as the bird of all knowledge, while the legends of many ancient cultures—Chinese, Egyptian, Greek, Semitic—depict it (perhaps harkening to Noah) as a foreteller of storms or bad weather.

There have been tame ravens in the Tower of London since the 11th century, and it is said that their loss or death will presage Britain's downfall. Superstitions were aroused during World War II when a rumour circulated that for five days not one Tower raven—including the customarily raucous newborns—had croaked. Another centuries-old legend holds that a raven's head buried on London's Tower Hill protects London from invasion.

Of all the world's peoples, none has shown the raven more attention or respect—or attributed to it a greater array of powers—than the Haida of the Queen Charlotte Islands on Canada's west coast. While many Haida stories depict the raven as a creature of supernatural power and wisdom, others depict it as meddling, lustful, greedy and foolish.

In the most reverent and audacious Haida tales, Raven is none other than the Creator, bringing humanity into existence, giving light to the dark world, founding lakes and streams, putting salmon in the streams and inventing tides. In one version of the Creation story, Raven, bored with the world as he has made it, gives genitals and sex to his creations—"Raven's greatest gift" as the legend depicts it. Always male, the bird is immortal and remarkably protean, able to re-invent himself in any form, from fish to leaf to rock or human being.

In another tale, Raven invites a host of birds to a feast, giving each a bright coat of paint to be worn for the celebration. During the feast, a ruckus breaks out, Raven gets agitated, and chases the birds away without washing off their paint. The mythic result is that, to this day, the birds wear their distinctive colours.

In tales less respectful to Raven, he is the "Trickster," a manipulator who entertains himself by drawing the creatures around him, including human beings, into elaborate ruses and deceptions. And he is lustful, sometimes turning himself into an irresistibly handsome young man to seduce the wife of an absent hunter or fisherman. His appetite for food is insatiable, as it would seem to be in nature.

Tales similar to those of the Haida are told in Siberia, which suggests that the stories came to North America—as did the Haida and other aboriginals—by way of the Bering Strait.

It is easy to see how the Trickster's identity evolved naturally out of the raven's tendency to imitate other birds or manipulate gullible animals so that it can steal their food. It is equally easy to see that the imagination that divined such an identity and gave birth to the ancient stories has been challenged and inhibited by the onslaught of new, perhaps less sensitive, cultures and ways. British Columbia artist Bill Reid points out in his book *Raven Steals the Light* that what remains of the original tales are mere scraps, dimly remembered fragments "frozen in museum attitudes." He also says that a flickering of the early spirit—of the artful imagination—is still evident in the homes and villages of the Haida.

If Raven is as wily and creative as he has been in the past (he would seem to have lost little of his edge in nature), and his human co-habitants are receptive, he may yet find a way to transcend the pressures of the contemporary world and revive that flickering spirit.

The Tree of Light

"The Tree of Light", which appeared in *Canadian Geographic* magazine in late 1994, attracted immediate criticism. A senior forester at Avenor pulp and paper, for example, was incensed at my saying that the ancient pine forest at Greenwood Lake—the focal point of the article—had survived the loggers' axes "by almost unaccountable fate." He felt that Avenor, which had at one time possessed cutting rights to the pines, should have had credit for its very "accountable" role in helping to preserve them, when under no obligation to do so. And it should have.

A local writer and silvaculturist was offended that I had chosen Dr. Will Carmean of Lakehead University's forestry department as one of my main sources of perspective on the preservation of old pine forests. Carmean, he pointed out, had once advocated (unsuccessfully) the use of a chemical weed killer on the lawns of Thunder Bay's Castlegreen housing cooperative, where both Carmean and the writer lived. How, he asked, could I trust anyone as a conservationist, who had once espoused this (seeming) ecological heresy?

The point was well taken by one who has never believed in the use of chemicals on lawns, and is mystified by the prevailing paranoia over dandelions. Given, however, that I knew nothing of the Castlegreen controversy at the time I wrote, I can say without irony or sarcasm that it was easy to trust Carmean. I can also say that even had I known about his advocacy of a particular weed killer at a particular time, in a particular situation, it would not have altered my perception of him as a thoughtful man who cares deeply about the fate of the white pine...and who catalyzed *my* caring, by introducing me to the pines at Greenwood Lake.

Truth is, anyone who says *anything* about logging or forest conservation in northwestern Ontario is apt to find himself in a quick and heated debate of a sort that too often plays out as an obtuse moral showdown between those who support the flattening of the forests and those who do not. I have friends on both sides of the issue and have made an effort to see their respective points of view. I accept the loggers' argument, for instance, that as a literate society we need paper, and therefore pulp, and must therefore cut trees. On the other hand, I am inclined to wonder if the "need" for paper encompasses endless Zellers' and Safeway flyers; or inch-thick Sunday newspapers, whose buyers, on average, are said to read less than one percent of what is printed outside of the front page and sports sections of those publications. I was told recently by a pulp-company executive that the packaging on a Kellogg's Variety Pac weighs as much as the cereal inside.

The arguments against trees for lumber are not nearly as intense as those against trees for pulp. Few would argue, for instance, that wood used as framing for houses was a waste of our valuable forests. Aluminum and synthetic framing are available, but the environmental costs of producing them almost certainly outweigh those of tree-felling.

It would be nice, if not hopelessly idealistic, to think that trees might eventually be cut and regenerated in ways that would allow habitat, soils and waters—and, of course, animal populations—to be preserved for the long haul.

It would also be nice to think that, just possibly, logging in this part of the country is more sound, ecologically, than it was in the days when men like my grandfather, a timber cruiser and lumberman during the late 1800s, wiped out the pine forests with an alacrity that beggars today's standards for environmental insolence. And perhaps things are better. Advances in reforestation and the protection of old growth forests might be construed as evidence of progress. In the meantime, the rain forests of Central America are being levelled with abandon. And giant cedars and firs on Canada's west coast are being felled not, as supposed, exclusively for the creation of fine lumber, but also so that phone companies in cities such as Los Angeles and San Diego can continue to supply customers with two or three copies of their 3000-page phone books

(most of the information in which could be distributed electronically over the phone.)

My purpose, however, is not to preach. Like Vancouver ecologist Andrea Schluter, I believe that if you want people to appreciate their environment you should avoid stultifying them with the grisly realities of environmental plundering and pollution, and introduce them instead to the pond, the woods, the meadow, and trust that a protective sensitivity will follow.

It is impossible to see the trees at Greenwood Lake and to come away without a sense that we should do what we can to ensure that such forests survive, and are renewed.

Having said that, I must allow that since seeing the trees at Greenwood Lake, I have done little or nothing to aid their survival—unless you want to count writing the article that follows. That's the easy part.

TO GET TO GREENWOOD LAKE, and to the 17th-century forest that rises off its south shore, you travel about a hundred kilometres west from Thunder Bay on Highway 11 and turn south on District Road 802. The latter, a once-vital logging route, has been allowed to deteriorate into a menacing succession of potholes, washouts and half-extruded boulders. It winds and bumps over granite outcrops, through beaver swamps, and across extensive cutovers long since cleared of jack pine and spruce for the pulp trade. These days, the road is better suited to moose, bear and lynx—all of which inhabit its precincts—than to human beings in motorized vehicles.

Yet to those with adventurous hearts and a craving for natural grandeur, it is a road of rich rewards. For, at a certain point perhaps thirty-five kilometres from the highway (it seems like seventy), the route crosses a basin of denuded lowland and climbs a shallow rise into one of the finest forests of old-growth white pine in North America. By almost unaccountable fate, these arboreal giants—approximately 10,000 of them on five square kilometres of crown land—have escaped the loggers' saws to grow as big and as old as nature has determined they should grow. Many of them are a metre or more in diameter and more than forty metres tall. Their fallen and rotting forebears, heavily covered in mosses, lichens, ferns and fungi, lie waist-high on the forest floor.

The sense of otherworldly magnificence imparted to anyone passing beneath these splendid trees is accentuated by the knowledge that many of them have been around for 300 years or more. Newton's Law of Gravity had barely gained acceptance when the first of them sprouted from the soil. By the time of the French Revolution in the late 1700s, most of them were thirty metres high and contained a thousand board feet of prime lumber. Not that there was anyone around who thought of them as fodder for the sawmill. The only people who had laid eyes on them at that point were wandering bands of woodland aboriginals who hunted and gathered in their shadows and happily shared them with black bears, eagles and warblers.

To say that the eastern white pine was common in those days is to utter an almost ludicrous understatement. At the end of the 18th century, the trees at Greenwood Lake were the merest fraction of the endless pine forests that shaded ridges and valleys from Newfoundland in the east to the southeast corner of Manitoba in the west; and from as far south as present-day Georgia to the shores of Lake Nipigon in northern Ontario. "It's entirely possible," says Dr. Willard Carmean, professor emeritus of forestry at Lakehead University in Thunder Bay, "that, in the early 1800s, someone could have travelled from the St. Lawrence Valley in Eastern Canada all the way to the centre of the continent and virtually never been out of sight of magnificent old pines."

Today, by comparison, trees such as those at Greenwood Lake are a rarity, a kind of ecological monument both to human folly and to their own fragile nobility. "Of all parts of the country, northern Ontario has the best of what's left of the old-growth white pines," says Carmean. "There are big fellas in Quetico Park and Temagami, for instance, and scattered stands off the north shore of Lake Superior. But you don't find many as old, as healthy or as dense as those at Greenwood."

It is a biological curiosity, and certainly more than a coincidence, that the Greenwood pines, all 10,000 of them, are virtually the same size and age. "It makes us think they took root after some catastrophic event, undoubtedly a major fire sometime during the late 1600s," says Carmean.

Far from being an enemy to the eastern white pine, fire is a

Will Carmean at Greenwood Lake.

necessity in the natural regeneration of the species. It not only lays bare the soil to receive seeds, but eliminates the dense understorey of brush and small trees, such as hazel, mountain maple and alder, so that the seedlings do not die from too much shade. Most mature white pines survive all but the worst fires thanks to their thick bark and to height that puts their crowns out of the reach of flames. "And even if the trees do burn," Carmean explains, "their cones will often survive, so that seeding can take place."

It is a sobering thought that, at some point in the foreseeable future, the splendid Greenwood pines will be gone from the face of the planet—lost not to the saw or axe but to the inevitable ravages of time and nature. Farther south, in the heart of the white pine range, healthy samples of the species might well be expected to live 450 years or more. But at Greenwood Lake, on the range's northern fringe, their maximum life span is thought to be reduced by as much as 100 years due to the shorter, colder growing season.

And yet as they live out their lives in the relative obscurity of the northwestern Ontario bush, these fine specimens are by no means reduced to biological museum pieces, deteriorating relics of the past. In 1992, the provincial Ministry of Natural Resources formally recognized the Greenwood Lake area as a "Scientific and Educational Reserve," protecting it as a kind of living laboratory for old growth research and education. As a result, a number of foresters and students, most of them from nearby Lakehead University, are quietly building data on regeneration, soil and biodiversity, as well as on birds and mammals with some unique relationship to the old-growth trees.

Research elsewhere has produced some fascinating insights into old-growth white pine ecology. One study by the United States Forest Service shows that when female black bears go off in search of food for their cubs, they invariably leave the cubs within a few metres of an old white pine if one is available. The particularly deep-fissured bark of the mature pine—as compared to the scaly bark of the jack pine or spruce, or the smooth bark of birch or poplar—allows the cubs to climb easily to safety should predators appear.

Because white pines tend to become hollow from rot in the latter stages of their life cycle, and then to topple, black bears also use them extensively as lodgings, squeezing into their interiors for an overnight snooze or a winter's hibernation.

A recently completed study in Superior National Forest in northern Minnesota revealed that during a thirty-one-year period, 77 percent of ospreys in the area built their nests in the crowns of old white pines, even though pines comprised a mere half-percent of the forest's larger trees. More than 80 percent of bald eagles used the trees for the same purpose. "They certainly can't build an 800- or 900-kilogram nest in a little spruce or poplar," says Carmean. (Some nests are used for decades, reaching immense proportions as successive generations of bald eagles add more and more nesting materials.)

The question is: when the grand old pines such as those at Greenwood Lake are gone, how much white pine will be around to replace them? Pessimists say not very much. The finest of the old-growth trees—and the respect they evoke for the species—

belie the fact that the eastern white pine, *Pinus strobus*, is a tree in significant trouble.

For one thing, it has been grossly over-harvested, particularly in the southern part of its range. More significantly, the natural regeneration of the species has all but ceased. There are so few young trees in existence, it is possible to walk through Greenwood Lake forest or Quetico Provincial Park and, with the exception of occasional saplings, not find a single healthy white pine under the age of 50 or 60 years. The reasons for this are well understood, but not so well that anything can be done to readily counteract them.

The species is, for example, an all but defenceless victim of the white pine blister rust, a hardy fungus introduced to North America during the early 1900s and gradually disseminated to the furthest extent of the white pine range. Spores from the fungus attack the needle clusters of the pine saplings and spread slowly along the branches to the trunk, where they choke off the sapwood, killing the tree. Mature trees—those that took root before blister rust entered the range—are relatively immune because their branches are above the height to which the airborne spores can rise.

If a sapling should escape blister rust, chances are it will fall prey to the white pine weevil, a voracious insect whose larvae deform young trees by killing their tender central leader. Again, mature trees tend to be immune because their branches are above the flying capabilities of the adult weevil.

Ironically, the most insidious of the tree's enemies is the very mechanism by which contemporary forests are intended to be spared: fire suppression. The white pine, to be blunt, would do better in a world of pyromaniacs than of honourable firefighters. "Up until the early 20th century, a forest fire could burn off hundreds, even thousands, of square kilometres of bush, and nobody much worried or did anything about it," says Bill Wiltshire," a forestry consultant formerly with the Thunder Bay branch of the Ministry of Natural Resources. "Today, we respond to every little fire that breaks out and douse it as quickly as possible. The result is that white pine doesn't achieve a whole lot of natural seeding."

While foresters have had lavish success in planting and growing species such as jack pine, red pine and white spruce, they have, in large part, failed in their attempt to plant and regenerate white pine. And in all probability they will continue to fail unless massive outlays of both effort and funding are directed toward the task. "The white pine's enemies are tough," says Carmean, "and the resources to fight them are in pretty short supply."

Not surprisingly, in recent years the species has taken on both ecological and totemic significance for conservationists, foresters and government resource agencies. "To say you're going to cut a white pine these days," says Wiltshire, "is about the equivalent of saying you're going to murder your mother. This is not just another species with a problem."

Historically, white pine has been a cultural, recreational and economic mainstay for residents of central and eastern Canada—not to mention a spiritual polestar for their native predecessors. For the ancient Iroquois it was the Tree of Peace, the roots of which were said to reach out to warring tribes in a symbolic plea for harmony. The Seneca considered it the Tree of Light, a link between the heavens and the earth.

Two-hundred-year-old pines en route to the mill near Nipigon in 1933.

During the early 20th century, the white pine emerged as a Canadian artistic icon, depicted by the Group of Seven in dozens of now famous canvases. For many, its vaguely oriental silhouette also became a symbol of the country's wilderness and recreational opportunities. Moreover it is the provincial tree of Ontario.

But it is in the realm of industry and economics that the white pine has made its biggest impact on Canadians, and vice versa. As early as 1810, agents of the British Crown were scouring the eastern forests, marking the tallest and straightest of the pines for use as masts, booms and spars on British ships. The Crown's traditional harvesting grounds in northern Europe had recently been cut off by the spread of the Napoleonic Wars into Germany, Russia and Scandinavia. What with tens of thousands of ships on the seas—and with some vessels carrying as many as six spare masts—the demand on the new supply was immense. At the time, the tree was commonly known as "mast pine."

As Canadian immigration and construction blossomed in the mid-1800s—and as ships turned increasingly to steam power— emphasis shifted to domestic use of the white pine. Looking back from the high-tech mesa of the late 20th century, it is difficult to

Pine logging in northwestern Ontario during the early days of the railway.

comprehend the surpassing significance of the white pine to 19th-century Canadians. For farmers it was a formidable obstacle that had to be removed from the land (and generally burnt) before crops could be sown. But for thousands it meant jobs in the bush camps, sawmills and finishing factories. And for millions it was a utilitarian treasure that affected them, quite literally, from (pine) cradle to (pine) coffin. It was framing and lumber for their homes, churches, barns and public buildings. Even brick and stone buildings were often erected around pine frames. Inside their homes, it was beds, tables, chairs, cupboards and dressers. What's more, it was the principal material of transportation, essential in the making of bridges, boats, wagons, railway cars and rail ties. It was mine timbers and wooden sidewalks.

At the forefront of the immense trade in pine were hundreds of boisterous logging camps in which the languages were many, the comforts and amenities few. In an average work day, there was little time in these frontier bivouacs for anything other than work, sleep and meals. And yet the lumberjacks who inhabited them, far from being mere brute labourers, were men of estimable skill and pride. A top notch "feller" could take down a giant pine, even in a wind storm it was said, and "land it on a tin plate." A good "top Decker" could build a wagon load of logs to such a height that it appeared to defy the laws of physics (on rare occasions gravity got the better of a load, sometimes leaving men and horses maimed or killed). The lumberjacks worked from sunrise to sunset, generally in the company of draft horses, oxen or, in one reported case, a team of domesticated moose. The animals were used to haul the logs to frozen waterways in anticipation of spring break-up and the log drive to the sawmills.

The industry was run by men entirely unburdened by concerns over the future of the forests. And why should they have been concerned? In the social and historic context of the their day, the nation-building in which they were engaged was a most admirable and honest calling—and a profitable one at that. The more trees they could cut and process, the better it was for everyone.

As a result of their ambitious work, the great pine forests of Eastern and central Canada had been all but flattened by 1920, and the pine harvest was moving inexorably north and west.

By 1940, the only old-growth forests still standing were those that had achieved some level of official protection—in provincial parks, for example, or in areas that were simply too difficult to reach with teams of horses. The forest at Greenwood Lake was among the latter. As the logging industry became increasingly mechanised through the mid-century, however, even isolated areas became relatively accessible to loggers.

Fast forward to a day in early March of 1994. At Inwood Forest Products—a lumber mill in Upsala, Ontario, 140 kilometres northwest of Thunder Bay—several hundred old-growth pine logs are stacked in the yard near the building in which they will soon be reduced to lumber. They are newly cut, and their exposed heartwood is the colour of liquid honey. Their sapwood glistens with pitch. Some show as many as 175 annual growth rings (anything over 120 is considered old growth). One by one, the logs are hoisted and taken indoors for their date with the saw.

Although no one planned it as such, this is something of a historic week at Inwood Forest Products. According to Jim Vibert, the logs in the yard might well be the last white pine the company will ever cut.

Vibert cut his first white pines in 1979, and throughout the 1980s exploited a profitable niche in the forest industry, harvesting limited pockets of mature pine left over from the heyday of the pine trade. "The big logging companies wouldn't have bothered with these trees," he says. "There wasn't a steady enough supply of them. But a mature white yields an average of 500 board feet of lumber, and a board foot wholesales for an average of 75 cents, so there was money to be made for a small operator like me."

The Ontario Ministry of Natural Resources regulates the cutting of timber on crown land, where virtually all of the province's commercial logging is done. After a review of forest inventory in 1989, the ministry advised Vibert that there was enough available white pine in the area to keep his mill operating profitably for twelve years, and that he was welcome to it. On these grounds he made investments that raised his company's debts to $1.5 million.

"Then in 1990," he says philosophically, "the naturalists and bird watcher, and so on, started putting pressure on the ministry to prevent loggers from cutting the old white pines. And almost before we knew it the ministry's policies began to change."

Stands of pine that Vibert had been given clearance to cut were suddenly off limits—"deferred," to use the ministry's term, until studies could be done to see whether cutting was advisable. the pine still available to him was in isolated locales that made harvesting uneconomical, or impossible.

"It wasn't that we ever cut all the pines in a stand anyway," says Vibert. "Regulations state that you have to leave two seed trees per acre. The best two. So, on average, we'd usually only cut two trees per acre."

By 1993, Vibert's business had shrunk dramatically. So had Upsala's economy, since many of the thirty people Vibert had employed off and on for years had been laid off.

Happily, the tale does not end there. At the urging of the ministry, Vibert had begun diversification with a new company called Upsala Forest Products, which will soon open a poplar-chipping mill to supply chips to the Avenor pulp and paper mill in Thunder Bay. The Upsala facility is expected to employ about a third of those laid off at the sawmill.

While Jim Vibert's story is the smallest of footnotes to the history of the eastern white pine, it is of genuine significance to the tiny community of Upsala. Moreover, it is at the heart of a fiery controversy that is an important chapter in the white pine's lengthy saga. Simply put, the controversy pits those who want to spare old-growth white pine against those who believe it can still justifiably be cut—ecology versus economy. Among the former are naturalists, environmentalists, educators, biologists, native groups, and those in wilderness tourism and recreation. The latter tend to be people whose livelihoods or social and economic well-being are affected by any decrease in pine logging.

"And there are lots of people between the extremes," says independent forester Bill Wiltshire. "I'm one of them. I tend to think, for instance, that in the Atikokan area, there's enough white pine to permit logging for a while yet, without any further damage whatsoever to the future of the species."

Vibert himself is somewhere in between—at least philosophically. "I think the forests are here for everyone—people, animals and plants included," he says. "And for future generations. I see the naturalists' point of view. I only wish they could see mine and allow me to use part of the forest for my purposes."

In January 1992, in an attempt to gain perspective on the old-growth issue, and to formulate a policy for the future, the Ontario Ministry of Natural Resources established an Old Growth Conservation Initiative and a Policy Advisory Committee. At the same time, much of the old-growth pine that had already been allocated for harvest by the ministry was put on "deferred" status.

In May 1993, after months of public consultation with people on all sides of the issue, the committee produced a report on both red and white pine (the red is in far less trouble than the white pine, because it has few natural enemies and is easily regenerated). The report includes the observation that the term "old growth" is not so much a description of the age of an individual tree as that of an ecosystem, an interactive group of plants and animals reflective of the forest before European settlement.

"The Ministry of Natural Resources has done a preliminary inventory of old-growth pine forests, but we need more information about their characteristics," says Carmean. "The committee's first recommendation was that a detailed inventory be taken. We not only want to know what stands are out there and roughly what age, but what condition they're in, what other species they're growing with, what their density is, and so on."

It is a process that will involve exhaustive perusal of existing forest maps and photos, as well as laborious on-site investigation by field staff. "You have to understand," says Wiltshire, "that when they say there's not much old growth left, they're speaking in relative terms. There are still millions of individual old white pines in Northern Ontario. Even in the heart of the range, where logging was heaviest, there are thousands of isolated trees 200 years old or more. And there's lots of second-growth stuff between, say, 75 and 100 years old. It all has to be sorted out."

Another of the committees recommendations was that representative old-growth stands be chosen and officially protected in a variety of geographical and climatic areas. "In northwestern

Ontario," says Wiltshire, "they'll be protecting roughly 20 percent of what's out there, which, added to the 30 percent or so already protected in provincial parks means roughly half the old-growth white pine in this region will be preserved." In all probability, limited logging will continue to be allowed.

It is of greater importance yet to the long-range survival of the white pine that representative stands of mid-age pine will also be protected under the new policy, assuring the existence of old growth long after present stands have fallen.

What's more, concerted efforts will be made to regenerate white pine—not just to plant it but to assist the young trees in surviving their formidable enemies. "If we're serious about old growth," says Carmean, "we have to be regenerating."

But can regeneration be accomplished on any significant scale? Nobody's quite sure. "It certainly can't be if we don't try," says Carmean. "I tend to be an optimist, and there are measures we could be taking to benefit regeneration."

One would be to develop a strain of white pine that is genetically resistant to blister rust. So far, however, attempts in that direction have failed. Another would entail meticulous, yearly, hands-on attention to the young trees, until they are big enough to fend for themselves: measure such as pruning away blister rust damage so that it doesn't spread; or eliminating nearby gooseberry and currant plants which are necessary co-hosts in the life cycle of the blister rust fungus. But measures of this sort would require massive annual commitments of labour and funding, making them highly unlikely candidates.

The most obvious possibility for regenerating young white pine—although results are by no means guaranteed—would be to plant seedlings in dry upland areas where the absence of humidity discourages gooseberry and currant plants, which thrive on moisture. The dry air would also reduce dew on the pines' needle clusters, making them less susceptible to blister rust. "At the same time," says Carmean, "if we were to encourage a light overstorey of, say, poplar or jack pine, these secondary trees would tend to

Left. There are some ten thousand 17th-century pines at
   Greenwood Lake.

protect the young pines from weevils. By the time the relatively short-lived poplar or jack pine died off, the white pine would be big enough to go it alone."

According to Glen Niznowski, a forester with the Kenora branch of the Ministry of Natural Resources, studies of white pine planted under such conditions during the past twenty to forty years reveal sporadic but identifiable success among the developing trees.

"I'd say we've got to start right now on this," says Carmean. "We'll never be able to regenerate enough to make white pine a significant industrial species again. But even as a secondary species, it's just so valuable that any investment we make will be worth it. And of course it has tremendous recreational and aesthetic value. And that doesn't begin to address what it means to wildlife and other plant species as it gets into its mature phase."

Which brings us back to the trees at Greenwood Lake. "They're a wonderful resource, a very special forest," says Carmean. "I never pass up an opportunity to go out and see them."

Carmean envisions a time when the Greenwood trees will be something of a magnet for ecotourism, and when anyone who wants to will be able to go out and see them. "What we don't want," he says, "is high-density recreational use—campsites, snowmobile trails, that sort of thing. Only good management is going to preserve this area." And, at that, only for a time.

"With some respect, some luck and some hard work, there'll be something around to replace those trees when they're gone," says Carmean.

Giving a tree with a great past a shot at a modest future.

❖

Secrets of the Gulch

My research for "Secrets of the Gulch" in the early summer of 1994 took me to one of northwestern Ontario's most exotic and inaccessible locales, the floor of Ouimet Canyon. In the months before the story's publication in November of that year, provincial parks officials in Thunder Bay voiced concern that, if the canyon's depths were given too much publicity in the article, increased numbers of hikers might be enticed to explore those depths on their own, which hikers are very much discouraged from doing. The prevailing caution is well-founded—the canyon is not a safe place to play. What's more, a number of rare plants that have survived in the canyon since the departure of the last glacier 10,000 years ago must be protected if they are going to survive. Given these concerns, I thought the least I could do was to avoid describing in print the route by which photographer Lori Kiceluk and I—and our hosts Cam Snell and George Holborn—got from the lip of the canyon onto its floor 110 metres below.

I have been asked since if we belayed down on ropes or went in by helicopter. While either method might have appealed to my secret self-perception as a superhero, the truth is, we scrambled inelegantly down a slippery narrow trail at a well-camouflaged point where the cliffs are less sheer than they are in most places along the canyon wall.

We went down at about 10 a.m. on a clear warm day, and when we emerged six hours later I was as drained as I'd have been had I spent the entire time breaking granite with a sledgehammer. Getting around in the bottom of the canyon is an endless game of leaping from one immense boulder to another, often at precipitous angles, as you stagger up and down the banks of fragmented rock that have crashed into the canyon over the centuries. There is not a metre of easy walking. Add to this that we were carrying far too little drinking water in an area that on a windy day can be as dry as Arizona, and a picture begins to emerge. The legs turn first to rubber, then to wood, and finally to concrete.

That morning, as we had hiked along the brink of the canyon to our point of descent, George Holborn, a provincial parks naturalist, pointed out to me that the young leaves of the clentonia plant—perhaps known best for its pretty blue berries—are both tasty and succulent to eat. The happy result of this was that as we emerged from the canyon parched and hungry I began immediately to gobble clentonia leaves, fifty or more of them, which succeeded temporarily in quenching my thirst and satisfying my hunger (for anyone inclined to such fodder, I might mention that the meal went stem to stern on me with mercurial speed). But the food did nothing for my weariness, so that when we stopped for ice cream at Pass Lake, on the way back to Thunder Bay, my fellow travellers could barely rouse me from the comatose stupor into which I'd fallen in the passenger seat of the Ministry of Natural Resources truck.

Why do I mention all this? Perhaps because the rebellious kid in me has never quite adjusted to being told what I ought to include in an article or leave out—or even to taking suggestions on such matters. But moreso to make the point that the orderly surface of a piece of writing often disguises the chaotic realities out of which the piece has emerged. I think it is true of most writers that we tend to remember the chaos long after the resulting sentences and paragraphs have faded from memory. For once, I'm happy to offer both.

LIKE ALL GOOD STORIES, the saga of Ouimet Canyon is a gathering of dramatic forces—some so delicate they would barely disturb the flight of the azure blue butterflies that inhabit the canyon's depths, others of a power that would fracture the crust of the earth.

Unlike most stories, the details and plot of the Ouimet saga depend more on who does the telling than on anything fixed in print. Ask a botanist about the canyon, and he'll describe an exotic garden of lichens, mosses and rare arctic flowers, some of them a thousand kilometres south of their normal range. A geologist will tell you about the mysteries of the canyon's beginnings—a Chinese puzzle of rock types, talus and glaciation.

Baby boomers who grew up in the region before the canyon became a provincial park in 1972 have quite another story to tell: "During the fifties and sixties, teenagers would drive out there and literally risk their lives, hanging over the edge, climbing down on ropes, all sorts of daredevil nonsense," says Teresa Celmer, who grew up in the nearby town of Red Rock on Lake Superior's north shore. "In those days you could drive right to the brink of the canyon. It was a thing to do on Friday or Saturday night. A couple of kids took cars up there and pushed them over the edge." (The Ontario Ministry of Natural Resources has long since hauled out the wreckage and cut off direct vehicle access.)

For the roughly 12,000 casual viewers who visit the canyon yearly, it is primarily a place of grandeur and of their responses to that grandeur: the queasiness that invariably accompanies the first tentative steps onto either of the two open viewing platforms on the canyon's west side; the white-knuckled grip on the rail; and, after the inevitable silence at seeing the spectacle for the first (or fortieth) time, the breathy expression of appreciation—"Wow!"

For the visitor who descends to the canyon's depths (permission is officially required, although apparently not always obtained), the place is yet another story, one not just of spectacle but of unnerving sensory distortion. The acoustics of the canyon are so extraordinary that, from the canyon floor, the tapping of a pileated woodpecker a hundred metres above takes on the frantic volume of machine-gun fire, striking the listener seemingly from all directions as it rebounds off the rock. the squawk of a raven at the canyon's upper edge is amplified in such a way that, on hearing it, a hiker, out of protective instinct, will throw his head back, alert, half expecting to see the bird within metres of his face.

"One morning in early summer about three years ago," says park superintendent Cam Snell, "We came out to check the viewing pods and, just as we got to the edge, a boulder broke free of one of the rock faces and fell into the canyon." Because the diabase in the canyon walls is so hard and the acoustics so resonant, the resulting crash made what Snell describes as a "high-pitched ceramic explosion, like a landslide of broken china...followed by a little cloud of dust rising off the canyon floor."

Even the wind, funnelling up the canyon from Lake Superior, four or five kilometres to the south, comes edged with a whistling agitated moan.

But the sensory warp at the bottom of the 110-metre-deep canyon is by no means limited to sound. As the hiker descends through varying thermoclimes, the temperature can change dramatically—from, say, 15C at the surface to 3 or 4C on the canyon floor. Because of the limited direct sunlight, a thick bed of ice exists year round beneath the massive boulders in the deepest part of the canyon. Isolated pockets of snow have been known to linger well into the summer.

Quite apart from all this, there is the intense, almost meditational isolation of the place, the sense that, in the depths of the canyon, you have entered some vast natural cathedral. The feeling is due largely to being cut off from the rest of the world by towering walls of solid rock. But part of it, too, is the age of that rock, 1.4 billion years, impossible to comprehend except as a kind of mantra for reflections on time and mortality, the ultimate insignificance of human endeavour.

Ouimet Canyon is situated just north of the Trans-Canada Highway, some eighty kilometres east of Thunder Bay. It measures 2.5 kilometres in length and varies between 60 and 200 metres in width. While its north end is a cul-de-sac, its south end opens onto thousands of hectares of boreal forest that slope gradually downward past tiny Gulch Lake to the shores of Lake Superior.

According to George Holborn, a regional naturalist with the Ontario Ministry of Natural Resources, the canyon derives its name from Lieutenant Colonel Albert Ouimet, who was discharged from Montreal with the Montreal Rifles in 1885 to help quell the Riel Rebellion in Manitoba. "This was at the same time that the CPR was being built, and the troops were travelling by rail," says Holborn. "But there were sections along Lake Superior

Ouimet Canyon during the 1920s.

that weren't yet completed, so part of their job along the way was to help put down rail." The hard-working colonel and his men were so well liked by the navvies and railway administrators that, when the time came to build a station in the area southeast of the canyon, the resulting whistle stop was named Ouimet. While the station has long since disappeared, the canyon and a minuscule community commemorate the colonel's name.

The canyon is reputed to have been a native trapping ground during the 1800s, although there is no proof of this. It is assumed that few if any natives actually lived in the immediate area, inasmuch as no cultural artifacts have ever been found on or around the site. In 1936, a local trapper named Alex Anderson told the Port Arthur/Fort William *News Chronicle* that aboriginal ghosts inhabited the canyon and that, while sleeping there one night, he had been visited by the ghost of a mythic chief who implored him to "guard the secrets of the gulch."

Dutiful to a fault, the trapper refused further comment on what those secrets might have been. "Certainly it's been speculated that the canyon had sacred significance to pre-European natives," says George Holborn. "All you have to do is look at it to see that it's a very powerful place."

It can also be a very dangerous place. Because of the extensive fracturing of the rock along the edges of the canyon, massive slabs of diabase are inclined to break off at irregular intervals, contributing to the deep slopes of broken rock in the canyon's depths. At a particular point along the west wall, the rock has broken off in such a way that a high, fragile pillar has been left standing, some ten metres out from the cliff face. Because the pillar's upper portions bear a chiselled resemblance to a high-cheekboned face, it has for decades been referred to as "the Indian head."

"I'm sure the thing's none too stable," says Cam Snell, "but nevertheless somebody risked his or her life climbing it a few years ago, to put a ribbon around the head. The ribbon was there a long time before it fell off."

In places along the upper edges of the canyon, where visitors once strolled, visible fractures have opened parallel to the canyon, within metres of the brink. Some of them are eerily deep, and wide enough to swallow an unwary human being. Eventually, freeze-thaw action will force them open to a point where they give way, and new slabs of rock will tumble. Park officials measure the fissures yearly to monitor their expansion and the associated risk. Officially, visitors are prohibited from wandering into such areas, and also from hiking into the canyon proper, except to do scientific or journalistic research. "There's just too great a danger of falling rock," says Snell.

There may also be a danger of falling projectiles. For some visitors, the temptation to pitch something, anything, into the gorge—rocks, sticks, logs, bottles, cans—is so strong that the once-verdant area beneath the south viewing platform is entirely denuded of foliage where various jettisoned objects have struck. "A while back, someone tore up an interpretive sign and the podium that supported it and threw it over the rail," says Snell. "The place just seems to do weird things to some people. It's as if they have no other way of relating to this sort of spectacle." During the 1960s, a Nipigon resident committed suicide by driving his car over the edge.

"A curious thing happened when we built the viewing pods

The canyon today. Brandon and Amy Celmer on the south viewing pod.

during the late eighties," says George Holborn. "Even though they made the place a lot safer, people from the area complained that we'd ruined the true experience of the canyon for them. They *liked* going right up to the edge without protection, getting down on their stomachs and leaning out over. We want people to realize that if they do come out here and hang over the edge, or go down into the canyon, they're doing it at their own peril; it's very risky."

To understand the formation of this place of grandeur and peril— inasmuch as it can be understood—it helps to know that the region, for hundreds of kilometres around, sits on a bed of relatively soft sedimentary rock or shale laid down by shallow mineral-laden seas nearly 1.5 billion years ago. It also helps to know that shortly after the shale was deposited, molten diabase, a much harder rock, was forced upward into the shale, settling throughout it in "sills," immense puck-shaped intrusions, some as wide as ten kilometres and up to 300 metres thick.

With the eventual erosion of the surrounding shale, many of the erosion-resistant sills were left standing on their own, some rising more than two hundred metres above the surrounding landscape. Today, their perimeters are defined by steep rock cliffs, their lower portions by embankments of "talus," accumulated boulders that have fallen from the rock faces over the millennia. An elongated series of these diabase sills forms the Sleeping Giant, a renowned landform at the tip of the Sibley Peninsula, visible from Thunder Bay. Others form low mountains along the north shore of Lake Superior between Duluth, Minnesota, and Schreiber, Ontario.

Ouimet Canyon cuts straight through one of these lofty diabase sills. What is known for certain about the canyon's formation is that, many millions of years ago, deep fractures or joints developed in the diabase. These may have been giant cooling cracks formed during the rock's solidification, or else pressure cracks formed when the sills warped as the softer rock underneath was compressed.

"But from there on it's a bit of a guessing game," says Maurice Lavigne, resident geologist for the Thunder Bay District of the Ontario Geological Survey. "The most common theory is that, through several glacial periods, ice and runoff invaded an existing system of these fractures in the diabase sill, gradually loosening the rock and creating an erosional channel. As millennia passed, the channel deepened and widened."

Park literature suggests alternatively that the great weight of glacial ice may have caused a downwarping of the edges of the sill, breaking it open along a fracture line in the middle, in effect snapping it like a biscuit, opening it to erosion.

"But I don't accept either of those theories," says Lavigne, who, in recent examination of aerial photos of the area, just may have hit upon the earliest "secret of the gulch." Lavigne suggests that early fracturing somehow loosened a segment of the sill comparable in shape to what he calls "a piece of pie."

"Along came the glaciers," he explains, "and gradually slid the piece of pie out of its original position." His theory concludes that displacement along one side of the pie segment became the main north-south axis of the canyon.

Glaciation was also responsible for the canyon's remarkable botanical legacy. "When the last of the Laurentide glaciers cleared the area some 10,000 years ago," says Holborn, "arctic plants that had thrived just beyond the glacier's cold southern fringes migrated north behind it, putting down roots in the newly deglaciated terrain." As conditions warmed, many of these species died off in the area, either from lack of a compatible climate, or from competition with boreal trees which were also following the glacier north. Certain arctic species survived, however, in what is now Ouimet Canyon, where the cold micro-climate suited them and where, because of the lack of soil, they were largely free from forest competition. "And there they exist to this day," Holborn says. "There are species in the canyon that normally don't grow south of Hudson Bay."

The most evident of these far northern species are the lichens, which crowd the surface of the rocks, where the cold, dry conditions match those of the tundra. "There are probably 150 species of lichen in the canyon," says Holborn. "If you get into the shaded microhabitats, under the boulders where it's really quite cold, you'll find very tiny, extremely rare crustose lichens."

The lichens, as a whole, make a massive subtle pallet of the canyon's walls and talus. Their colours range from varying grays and browns, through white, black, pink, even luminescent yellow, to the bright orange *caloplaca*. Recent rock falls and talus slides are easily identifiable because of the lichen-free rock.

Among the floral species, perhaps the prettiest is the arctic pyrola, *Pyrola glandiflora*, a species of arctic wintergreen that grows amid damp mosses in the deepest parts of the canyon. The plant's pinkish or greenish flowers, each about as big around as a nickel, bloom in a cluster during July and August atop a single stem ten to fifteen centimetres high. The shaggy moss, *Aulacomnium acuminatum*, and the liverwort, *Temnome setiforme*, also flourish is the canyon, hundreds of kilometres south of their normal range.

Along either side of the canyon, where the talus slopes meet the cliffs, a band of almost comically dwarfed birches, cedars and spruce is rooted precariously in whatever cracks and crevices hold a modicum of soil. In some cases, the stunted trees exhibit an arboreal phenomenon known as "layering," by which a branch has somehow come into contact with surrounding terrain and set down roots of its own. This often occurs where trees are deprived of nourishment, and lead to the establishment of new trees genetically identical to the parent. "As much as anything visible," says Holborn, "these tenacious little trees are an image of the canyon's brutally tough climatic and growing conditions."

They are also evidence that the story of Ouimet Canyon is rich in the arcane subtleties of the natural world. "There are some very complex things going on here," says Holborn.

And yet the average visitor to the canyon is probably less concerned with fine points of botany and geology than with what Cam Snell calls "a larger, more spectacular sense of the place."

"What most people want when they come to Ouimet would seem to be something fairly primal," says Snell. "And it's great if they can get it just by stepping out onto one of the viewing pods, looking around and absorbing the spirit of what's here. It's not the sort of sensation you can get everywhere.

"Then again, it's terrific if visitors are inspired to pick up on some of the history or botany or geology. Like all parks, this one is what people make of it."

Measured against Niagara Falls, the Rocky Mountains or the tides of Fundy, Ouimet Canyon is not one of Canada's more conspicuous natural splendours. Yet those who make time for it as they travel the Trans-Canada east of Thunder Bay invariably sense that, like the mountains and tides, it is a story worth knowing and worth telling...in any or all its various versions.

❖

Thunder Bay:
More Personal and Better Imagined

If I can offer anything in the way of a preamble to what follows—a story that, more than any in the book, introduces and explains itself—it would be a brief but sincere thanks to my friends at CBC radio—in particular Fred Jones and, more recently, Carmen Klassen—who, over the past five years, have given me an open ticket to wander the city, then go into the studio and talk about my wanderings on the air. It's been a pleasure and has shown me a multitude of images of Thunder Bay that I would never have known otherwise.

D URING JULY OF 1990, I was commissioned by a Canadian magazine to travel to Thunder Bay for a few days and, based on what I saw and heard, produce a 4,000-word article—a so-called "in-depth" feature—on the city.

I arrived, as I recall, on a Friday morning, zonked with a summer virus, checked into the Prince Arthur Hotel, and slept for the better part of forty-eight hours. I spent Sunday touring the city in a rented Crown Victoria (air conditioner and tape deck blasting), and on Monday morning interviewed the Mayor, Jack Masters, and the manager of the Visitors and Conventions Department, Pat Forrest. During the afternoon, I cruised the waterfront with Cy Cook of the Harbour Commission, visited a Manitoba Pool elevator, and, out of nostalgia, drove to Kakabeka Falls where, as a teenaged hitchhiker, I had spent a rainy night stranded under a picnic table in the provincial park. On the way back to town I drove to the lookout on Mount McKay but was unable to see the city for haze.

I spent another day in bed, interviewed a band councillor from the Fort William Reserve, and, without doing much else, packed my bags and flew home.

The article appeared the following February under the title "East Meets West at Thunder Bay," accompanied by the sub-head: "Declining grain shipments have forced the Lakehead city to diversify...and fast."

The piece might better have been called "Where the Ding-dong Rings and the Dicky Bird Sings," inasmuch as it was full of the sort of nonsense that could only have been perpetrated by someone whose optimal take on the city had been achieved from the mists of Mount McKay, or in sleep at the Prince Arthur Hotel. Which, under certain circumstances, might have made for an interesting story.

Unfortunately, much of the piece was as dull as tanker bilge. At its core was a stultifying analysis of the shrinking grain trade, stuff you could read, and read again (actually, it would have been excruciatingly difficult to read it even once), without remembering so much as a syllable... stuff that I suspect will be on hand as counter-evidence when I try to convince St. Peter that I have attempted to live honourably and have used well what talents I have.

The piece included pronouncements so idle and flattering to the city they must surely have caused blushing even at the local propaganda mill. "The city's excellent arts facilities," declared one airless sortie, "are rivalled, if not surpassed, by an array of recreational and tourist facilities, including a first-rate downtown marina, a multi-use athletic complex built to host the Canada Games in 1981, five local ski hills, and cross-country and snow-mobile trails. The surrounding wilderness attracts campers, hikers, hunters and fishermen from all over the continent."

At one point, I noted with authority that "Hawks and herons cruise the city's skies; moose and bear are often seen wandering its streets."

Mercifully, there were also paragraphs that lent a modicum of texture and authenticity to the story. Rereading it, I am far from chastened, for instance, to read Bill Climie's detailed account of how, on the day after the Americans dropped the first atomic bomb in August, 1945, grain dust ignited in Saskatchewan Pool's Number 5 elevator on the Port Arthur waterfront, blowing the place up, killing some twenty workers and injuring dozens. "I was a student working for Sask Pool that summer," Bill told me. "That morning I was on the top floor of the Whalen Building, when we were shaken by this terrible boom. My dad, who was a foreman, was in Number 4 elevator at the time, and the explosion blew his phone off the wall—it hit him in the face and broke his cheekbone. When we heard the blast, it was as if another bomb had been dropped."

Nor am I unhappy with the account of how an annex of the city's northernmost grain elevator, a United Grain Growers facility, toppled sideways into Lake Superior on a mild evening during September, 1959, taking with it two million bushels of wheat and sending a twenty-foot tidal wave over the adjacent shipyards. My source on the story, Stan McKay, who managed the elevator at the time, explained to me that a crew of men who had been painting the elevator had taken down their scaffolding that afternoon, and that a ship that was supposed to have been loading grain during the evening had decided to wait until morning. "Oh, it was a sight," he said. "If the men had been painting, they'd have been gone. If the ship had been in, it would have been buried."

I am happy, too, to have met Jack Masters, who gave me a copy of Joseph Mauro's popular history of the city, from which I gleaned much of what commentary I included on the past.

By and large, however, my take on the story seven years after the fact is one of embarrassed dismay, combined with a vague desire to make amends for depicting the city so tediously and with such obvious disregard for the evidence (subtle disregard for the evidence is a writer's prerogative).

Had I not moved to Thunder Bay six years ago I would never have known. But I did…and during those years have had ample opportunity to form a more vivid, and I would hope more accurate, impression of the city—at very least a more personal and better imagined impression (reality, the mystic said, must be imagined before it can be perceived).

Given the opportunity to imagine it again, I would include among other references…

◆ The view from the window at which I sit writing—a panoramic sweep of old mountains, deep forests and perhaps a hundred square kilometres of the planet's most majestic and mysterious body of water. In the near distance: sailboats, ships, gulls, terns, ravens…the

Thunder Bay and its grain elevators viewed from Hillcrest Park.

lighthouse and breakwater. In the background, the bay and the
Sibley Peninsula. At night, the lights on the ships at anchor look
like villages on a distant plain. I have seen the bay in almost every
colour of the spectrum, including blue, mauve, white, grey, silver... red and orange at dawn, and a bright greenish turquoise as the
ice was going out last spring. The other day, as I glanced from my
work, I saw the Bluenose II tacking up the bay under full canvas.

◆ I would name the bridges on Main Street and Central Avenue,
because it is from these two high points that you get the essential
view of Thunder Bay—every major structure and landform visible, in all directions. The bridges are not the sort of places that
most people ever get to on foot, but the advantage of walking
them is that you can stop at their summits and just look—at the
mountains and ski runs; the elevators, mills and office buildings;
neighbourhoods, churches, parks; islands and waters; schools
from K to PhD. You can peer into the railyards, where, on the
various sidings and lines, you can sometimes count as many as
800 cars, most brimming with wheat, lumber or logs, but some
with more mysterious cargoes. One morning last fall, I watched
nine consecutive gondola cars pass beneath me, each full of what

could only be described as orange-painted cannonballs, some the size of melons, others no bigger than plums—presumably travelling from the smelter to the steel mill or foundry. From the Main Street bridge at dusk, you can watch the deer come out of the poplar woods to the east to feed on the grain along the tracks. I have seen as many as thirty-two of them, and have seen a dozen or more ravens feeding, in turn, on an unlucky doe. What's more, you can *hear* the city from the bridges: crows, ravens, gulls, the roar of trucks and the clang of the train engine bells…and always in the distance the persistent rumble, sometimes just a hum, of wheel and rail. One evening, the sudden crash of boxcars beneath me sent several hundred pigeons flapping onto the sunset. Depending on the wind, you can smell creosote, sawdust, spruce bark and malt—and, particularly from the Main Street bridge, the sweet fermenting sludge of wet grain.

◆ I would name old-world retailers such as Maier Hardware, where you can buy anything from a woodstove to a single finishing nail; and Pittarelli's Shoe Rebuild, with its gleaming antique machinery. Pasquale Pittarelli learned shoemaking as a boy in the Campobasso region of Italy and has taught enough of the business to his daughter, Mary, that when necessary she can run the place on her own… And the Vienna Bakery, where owner Joe Krebs and his son Al, two of the pleasantest guys in Port Arthur, turn out excellent rye bread and, for a fee of $20, will roast you a pig in the big Pendrith oven. I would mention Maltese's Italian Foods and Ziggy's Sports Exchange.

And Lauri's Hardware on Bay Street, the Smithsonian of hardware stores. The inventory at Lauri's encompasses items you'd never have known are still being manufactured: spittoons, chamber pots, scythes, kerosene lamps, galvanized watering cans, washboards, cant hooks, axes made specifically for cutting cedar shakes…plus thousands of more prosaic items, such as fish smokers, blueberry pickers and cast iron cooking pots, some as big as car tires and weighing a dozen kilos or more. The store sells ice axes and machetes and a gazillion kinds of knives.

Lauri's is also a pawn shop, with a mouldering reserve of unclaimed bowling balls, typewriters, jewellery and VCRs, anything you can think of, all of it for sale.

Lauri, the owner, is 72 years old, round in the middle, and has the face of a Lapland gnome. He retired from the clothing business in 1975, but, as he puts it, "couldn't stand the pace of retirement," so opened the hardware store a year later. "I'm strictly no-bullshit," he says of his pricing system—meaning, most evidently, that he prefers to deal cash and that all prices are rounded to the nearest dollar, tax included. "Gimme ten bucks," he says when asked about the price of a jackknife. "How much to cut a key?"... "Gimme two bucks."

One of the enduring features of the store is the little klatch of oldtimers who, in varying numbers, inhabit the area around the cash register, chattering away in Finnish, at any time of morning or afternoon. On a recent visit, I asked Lauri how many of them came in, and he looked at me astonished and said, "All of them!"

The secret about Lauri's these days—a mystery known only to several thousand of the owner's closest friends—is that if Lauri could find a buyer he'd be happy enough to pass the place along. When he revealed this to me, in strictest confidence, I said, "How much do you want for it?"

Mary Pittarelli and her dad Pasquale repair everything from purses to goalie pads to saddles at Pittarelli's shoe repair shop on Miles Street.

"For you personally?"

"No, for anybody."

"For anybody, I dunno—for you personally, I like you, you're a good guy, and you're probably gonna be out of work soon like everybody else—you'd look good in a place like this."

"How much do you want?"

"Gimme a hundred and fifty thousand," he said quietly. "No bullshit."

Lauri once explained: "I come in in the morning, I turn on the lights, and I think, 'I've got everything here that anybody could ever need.'... Except of course the things I don't have. And those I order."

◆ I would name the old neighbourhoods—among them, Westfort, the East End, Current River, the Bay-Secord-Cornwall area... On a fiery cold day in mid-December, 1995, I went down to the East End to gather notes for a broadcast I was to make the following week on CBC radio. The area is the oldest part of the city, the site of the original Fort William and, through the early years of the

Baker Al Krebs and his sister Liane Strocen grew up helping their dad, Joe, at Vienna Bakery on North Cumberland Street. Today, Al and his dad are well known for their European breads and pastries.

Lauri Hietala behind the counter at Lauri's Hardware on Bay Street. "What Lauri's doesn't have in hardware you really don't need!!!" says the well-known retailer's business card.

century, a kind of cauldron for Italian, Polish, Ukrainian and Slovak immigration. It was called "the Coal Docks," because the city's coal was unloaded along the north side of the Kaministiquia River, which is the southern boundary of the neighbourhood.

I was interested, among other things, in the three old Catholic churches clustered around Connolly and McIntosh streets, an enclave once referred to as "the little Vatican" and still a kind of axis of East End life. As I walked along Connolly Street past the Slovak Catholic Church, an elderly man in a stylish fur hat came gingerly up the street toward me. "Hello, Sir," I said. "Could I ask you a few questions about the East End?"

"Go ahead," he said amicably. "I've lived here seventy years."

We chatted briefly, and when I was about to say good-bye, he said, "Why don't you let me show you around? I'm legally blind, but if you'll let me take your arm, I'll t . fine."

And thus I toured the cradle of the city, arm-in-arm with Johnny Zack, who until recently had owned Zack's meat and grocery store on Pacific Avenue, founded in 1919 by his father.

We went first to the railyards and the site of the old fort by the river, where, at John's request, I read aloud the inscription on the granite monument commemorating the activities of the furtraders. Then, hunched against the wind, we tramped the streets, most of them named for the Scottish officers of the North West Company of furtraders... past the site of the old Belluz Winery... Covello's pool hall... Rocky Presidente's barber shop... the abattoir, the stock yards, the (Italian) Workers' Co-op, Purity Bakery, and the Fort William Broom Company, which at one time had a contract to supply brooms to the CPR. John explained that, during the early days, when a ship came up the Kam, the captain and officers would beat it over to Rocky Presidente's for a haircut, but that they were often so short of time that they had to buy their way into line by paying for the haircuts of everyone ahead of them.

At one time, John recalled, there were five bakeries and six skating rinks in the East End, an area not much bigger than the average nine-hole golf course. The immigrants would arrive from Italy or Eastern Europe, find living space in the boarding houses if they were single, or in drafty, ill-heated frame houses if they had families. They raised children and kept gardens, and at night listened for the whistles of the incoming ships, which brought many of them hustling to the docks for work. Those in more affluent parts of the city viewed the area with contempt, dismissing its inhabitants as a kind of lesion on the character of the city, necessary only in the enactment of the Empire's dirty work. "It was a lot of malicious nonsense," protested John. "The East End was a peaceable, thriving, bustling, vigorous community. It was one of the best neighbourhoods in the city, and it still is."

◆ For its poetry, I'd note the name of the city itself, with its resonant hints both of lake and land... and of our historic foundations in timber, mining, railways and ships, thunderous industries all. It is said that when the selection of a name was being considered during the months before amalgamation in 1970, the majority of citizens wanted to call their new city "The Lakehead" rather than Thunder Bay, both of which had been proposed. A rumour persists that the civic powers so favoured the latter that, when the issue was put to a plebiscite, they intentionally split the opposition vote by including the name "Lakehead" on the ballot, in addition to "The Lakehead." Whatever conniving might have taken place, they got the result they wanted (and democracy was, perhaps, justifiably sabotaged).

◆ Thunder Bay hasn't preserved a wealth of old architecture, but it has its share of intriguing buildings, a few of which I'd note for whimsical as much as architectural reasons. I am partial, for example, to the teetering hulk that is the Woodside foundry by Marina Park, and the former Bank of Commerce building on Victoria Avenue (which appeals to me, in part, because the fat pillars that hold up its portico bear an uncommon likeness to four huge cobs of corn)…and to the magnificent old machine shop at the shipyards…and the Brodie Library and St. Andrew's Church…and all the old institutions around Waverley Park…and of course the Whalen Building, with its creamy terra-cotta and marble, and reassuring solidity.

Like others, I feel an unresolved ambivalence toward the Ontario government building a few doors south of the Whalen. There are days when it seems so pretentious, uninviting and

Gardening has, for decades, been a mainstay of East End summer life. John Tomyn shows off the champion beans in his garden on McBain Street.

unforgiving as to be almost entirely at odds with what is best (and perhaps neediest) in the human spirit. On other days, its rawness and elegance seem perfectly to corral and echo the strength of the lake and the surrounding landscape.

I have no such ambivalence about the Brodie Library, which I admire, among other reasons, for its gracious windows, as attractive as any in the city, and for the stained-glass portraits that constitute the uppermost arches of those windows. Each of the latter depicts a pre-20th-century author, looking out at the world, or into it, with a frosty, five-mile stare: Goethe, Tolstoy, Shakespeare, Longfellow, Goldsmith, Dickens, Burns, Sir Walter Scott...and a guy named Moore, whose unadorned surname is emblazoned beneath his pinched puss, and who I had to look up in the reference books to peg as the Irish/English novelist George Moore. There are notably no women among the portraits—no Jane Austen, Mary Shelley, "George" Eliot, or Bronte sisters. The least that can be said about this omission is that the library was built in another era, in many ways a less democratic and sensitive era. So, there the women aren't—in a library whose top brass (as of this writing) are almost exclusively female.

The Ontario government building: warmer than Lake Superior but not by much.

The Brodie Library, (formerly the Fort William Public Library) was financed in 1906 with money from the Andrew Carnegie Foundation. At the time of construction, many Lakehead residents considered the Carnegie money tainted, because of the famous tycoon's ruthlessness towards non-unionized labourers in his American steel plant.

My fondness for St. Andrew's Presbyterian Church on Donald Street is, again, a response largely to windows—but also to the sumptuous little palace of its interior, which seems to have been carved whole out of, I guess, oak. The newer windows, installed during the 1970s, incorporate rough-hewn chunks of jewel-like glass, in memorably vivid reds, oranges, mauves and greens. A plaque outside draws attention to the polished granite columns that were erected with the rest of the place in 1908 to hold up the entrance arches—and which, in my opinion, bring an unfortunate hint of the crypt to the otherwise attractive portals with their leafy sandstone embellishments.

There are certainly no embellishments on the capacious old machine shop at the Port Arthur Shipyards. But, again, there are windows here that make it one of the more remarkable structures in the city. It is one of two big buildings left at the yards, and the daylight enters it through thousands of overhead panes, creating an illumination similar to what you see in the paintings of, say, Rembrandt or El Greco. Light doesn't so much brighten the space as press at the darkness without ever quite eliminating it. Depending on the angle at which the sun is coming into the shop, you get a striking interplay of light and darkness and shadow—and of course free-ranging layers of factory dust.

It was in this shop (and others now gone) that the shipyard produced the makings of its historic corpus of freighters, corvettes, minesweepers, tugs and ferries—one hundred and twenty-nine of them in all, some still afloat, some in Davy Jones' locker. There is still, among the shop's massive machines, a lathe the size of a Greyhound bus, and, in the adjacent fabrication shop, a 150-ton press that can fold up a piece of inch-thick steel plate as easily as if it were a handkerchief.

From its earliest days, in 1911, the shop also produced, among other commodities, paper-making machinery, dredge buckets, institutional boilers, furnaces, aircraft parts, store fixtures, shell casings—almost anything that suited its manufacturing and marketing capabilities. In the early 1930s, the company's electrical superintendent, Fenton Ross, designed a gothic-looking four-sided clock called a SporTimer. The shipyards built several of them, one of which hung for more than thirty years in Maple Leaf Gardens, another in the Montreal Forum—perhaps the most famous clocks in Canada. Fenton's original scale model is among the prized possessions at the Northwestern Ontario Sports Hall of Fame in Thunder Bay.

◆ There are so many things you could say about the waterfront: the elevators and saw mills and trains…the comings and goings of the ships…the Keefer Terminal (somewhat underused these days, but considered by shippers to be among the finest port facilities anywhere)…the tug docks and parks: Marina and Chippewa, and the smaller parks on Mission Island and at the mouth of the Floodway.

Mission Island, in the estuary of the Kam River, is a geographical anomaly, more like rural New Jersey than rural Thunder Bay, in that it brings together such an odd assortment of industry and junk pits and detritus with the beauty and fecundity of the coastal marsh and shoreline. The first thing you see as you cross the access bridge, for example, is the Lakehead Scrapyard where a three-storey shredder is in the constant process of turning rusty appliances and car bodies into a Vesuvius of rusty steel wool. The road leads out past Port Arthur Lumber, past a variety of derelict businesses, hydro facilities and towers, boat yards, ship-loading cranes...you go past all this, turn a corner or two, and, presto, you're back in Eden, at the waterfront, on the marsh, with its extraordinary view of the Sleeping Giant. When you look out at the Giant from the other end of the city, say at Marina Park, it gives you a sense of accessibility, in large part because it is the closest thing you see across the water. But at the Marsh, the Welcome Islands intervene, putting the Giant in the background, where it's as remote as Antarctica, way out there beyond the deeps.

Another of my waterfront interests is the nameless little settlement of Metis squatters who live in cabins made of lumber scraps, just south of the Richardson elevator. For years, I peered in there every time I passed in the car, occasionally spotting an inhabitant

Marina Park and four North Ward landmarks: the Ontario government building (centre), the old CNR station (right foreground), The Prince Arthur Hotel (behind station) and the Whalen Building (right rear).

or two—cutting wood, building, or, in summer, fishing or just sitting in their lawn chairs by the water. Then one day last February, I ventured in, ignoring a hand-lettered sign: METIS LAND— WHITE MAN KEEP OUT. Sweet-smelling woodsmoke rose from at least two of the cabins' chimneys as I padded along the sawdust entry lane, and I had a strong sense of being observed, although I could see no one, and was unable to raise an answer at any of the three doors on which I knocked. I stood for a minute looking around, then, feeling increasingly intrusive and uneasy, retreated down the path, my admiration for these latter-day survivalists undiminished.

I am a more frequent visitor at Dock 5, just south of Marina Park, where I go for no other reason than to see what the tugboats, the harbour's other resident survivalists, are up to. I was talking recently with Roland Frayne, who co-owns the city's largest tug, the *Point Valour*, which docks by Sask Pool elevator #7, and he told me, among other things, that when a tug goes out onto the bay to guide a ship into the harbour the fee for service can be as high as $1500, then another $1500 when the ship leaves. The tugs are by no means stylish craft, but they are shapely, and no matter how ravaged they get, they never seem to lose the good-natured innocence and likability that comes with their bright paint and jaunty little bridges and portholes…and of course their unimpeachable work habits.

Unfortunately, there is nothing innocent or likable about their neighbour at Dock 5, the partially demolished Saskatchewan Pool grain elevator, Thunder Bay's rotten tooth, which, for way too long, has been permitted to compromise the shoreline, not to mention the efforts of Tourism Thunder Bay whose people work overtime to sell the city as a tourist destination. The same might be said for the massive accumulation of creosote that has inhabited the harbour bed for how many decades. The so-called "blob" (now in the process of being contained by an enormous "berm") doesn't hurt the view but can't have done much for the quality of the water during the years of wrangling over which agency or industry was responsible for its treatment or removal.

One thing seems sure: If the removal of the Blob had been a matter of economy, not of mere health or integrity, it is all but certain that some combination of agencies would have been on the scene to deal with it as quickly as they were to vaporize Big Thunder when it suited their financial statements to do so.

◆ I am perhaps being frivolous in crossing environmental perils with recreation, but in my moment of irritability, I might just as well pause to lodge a grievance over the disappearance of high-level ski-jumping from the city. Once we had it, now we don't. And in its memory, I wish to say that it is difficult to think of anything in the realm of sport or entertainment more dramatic than the sight of a first-rate ski-jumper as he or she comes off the in-run and describes that incredible trajectoral arc down the mountain. It occurred to me one day as I stood at the top of the 120-metre jump at Big Thunder, marvelling at the courage of anyone who'd actually descend the thing, that the sport must surely be the high point in humanity's centuries-old struggle to overcome gravity and to fly unassisted. Leonardo himself worked on the problem, but it never occurred to him to do what the cagey Nordics did and put the wings on the feet.

Even the mention of ski-jumping reminds me of the excitement and enjoyment so many of us shared when the Nordic World Championships were held at Big Thunder in 1995. Nearly three years after the fact, I retain almost photographic recall of the 120-metre jumping on the last afternoon of the games, the event undecided, three jumpers left, each with a chance at the gold. First came Weissflog of Germany, a former world champion, who under pressure launched an inspired jump that propelled him into what everyone believed was an unsurpassable lead. Then came Goldberger of Austria, with a jump that beat even Weissflog's, and put him into the lead. The last jumper was a 17-year-old kid named Tommi Ingebrigtsen who had the (fading) hopes of Norway, not to mention of the local crowd, riding on his skinny shoulders. Down the run he came, ninety kilometres an hour, off the cliff, into the flight position… from the crowd of perhaps 20,000 there came first a kind of murmur, then a gasp that became, finally, a sustained roar, as the young Norwegian soared past Weissflog's mark, past Goldberger's, and so far on down the hill that I remember a sudden fear that he wouldn't be able to pull out of it and was going to crash onto the flats at the bottom.

He did pull out of course—but not until he had gone a good deal further than anyone had gone before on that hill.

There was a sense as we left the grounds that afternoon not only of wistful relinquishment for what we'd enjoyed over the past ten days (it was an event, incidentally, that put our own reluctant city in front of forty million television viewers around the world) but also of great satisfaction that in that last phenomenal jumping event, we had seen the best we were going to see.

What we didn't know of course was that we had also seen the last we were going to see, at least in Thunder Bay.

There is no local blame to be laid for the closing of Big Thunder, which, for the most part, was federally and provincially funded; but that doesn't make the loss of ski-jumping, or the awful waste of such a fine facility, any less palatable.

◆ Big Thunder, it should be said, is part of the Nor'Wester range of mountains, clearly visible from downtown Thunder Bay and certainly deserving of a place in any piece of writing on the city. The range hugs the uppermost curve of Lake Superior, extending southwest along the Slate River Valley, toward the U.S. border. It is among the oldest mountain groups on earth and is one of Canada's most distinctive landforms. I have driven along logging roads into the Falling Snow area in Pearson Township, southwest of the city, up onto Twin Mountains, where the view, as my friend Scot Kyle once described it, is like something out of the peyote dreams of Carlos Castanada. Highway 61 takes you more or less through the heart of the range, then across the border and along the Minnesota shore of Lake Superior, with its long views, long birches, and its beaches of smooth pinkish stones.

◆ Which brings me to a point where I would do well to mention that Thunder Bay is located at the crux of a "T" formed by two mythic roads, the afforementioned Highway 61, which John Steinbeck referred to as "the back bone of America," and our own legendary Trans-Canada, which, as much as the lakes, woods and rocks, is a fundamental of life in northwestern Ontario. For my money, no highway in the country—not the Cabot Trail on Cape Breton Island or 93 Highway between Jasper and Banff—is more dramatic than the stretch of the Trans-Canada that connects

Sault Ste. Marie to Thunder Bay. I have driven the highway so many times in so many kinds of weather, in every month of the year, and have experienced so many of the highs and lows it can dish out, that it has become for me a kind of paradox, an image both of my freedom (and the implied freedom of the wilderness) and of something more sinister, in that three times over the past four years I have come within a hair's breadth of losing my life on its pavement or right-of-way. I survived a moose in '93, a rock-cut in '95 and, on a night last winter, an all-but-impassable blizzard as I drove in from Nipigon where, earlier in the evening, a cadre of the (very very) faithful had gathered at the public library to hear me read from my work.

Because it is the right of every citizen of northwestern Ontario to relate an occasional Trans-Canada nightmare—and because it verges on regional fable—I shall describe in the briefest terms how, a few kilometres east of the Pass Lake cut-off, a transport whisked by me, forcing me ever-so-slightly onto the shoulder to the right...and how, under the fatally icy conditions, even my most delicate manoeuvre to pull all tires back onto the road turned out to be an overcompensation, so that suddenly there I was doing 360s down the middle of the highway as Bob Marley howled from the tape deck and another 18-wheeler came over the hill toward me some four hundred metres away. I remember thinking as I spun that if I had enough momentum to continue across onto the far shoulder I might not die. Otherwise, there was a sense that I had already departed.

I remember more clearly the elation as my back wheels touched gravel through the deepening snow, and I knew at least that I was not going to come to rest in the oncoming lane—a feeling quickly supplanted by the realization that I was still moving at sufficient speed to travel clear across the shoulder and over the edge of the steep, unprotected embankment beyond.

Suffice it to say that I came to rest with my rear wheels hanging a good half-metre over the edge...and that for the next five hours, I sat there in the blizzard, unwilling to walk for fear of freezing, unable to stop a transport, yet jumping from my vehicle as each one passed, so as not to get walloped if it lost its traction (as it certainly would have if it had tried to brake).

It was not until dawn, when the snow stopped and the wind died, that I was able to hitch a ride into Pass Lake.

My adventures on the Trans-Canada have shown me almost every kind of mammal in the boreal forest: bears, moose, deer, lynx, porcupines, foxes, wolves, skunks, beaver, muskrats…and a host of smaller creatures. It is my privilege to believe that, on a crisp December morning, in 1994, near Dorion, I saw a cougar cross the road perhaps two hundred metres in front of me. I have been told by all and sundry that my imagination was undoubtedly working overtime and that what I probably saw was a dog…a house cat…a pony…or perhaps just a road-devil or snowmobile. But the fact remains that I know of no other animal, and certainly no machine, with a four-foot tail and a head the size of a basketball.

I have seen herons, owls and perhaps more vultures than I care to acknowledge. I have also seen an impressive sampling of the country's geology, and have begun in recent years to pick up stones, some quite large, from the beaches and rock-cuts between the Soo and the Manitoba border some 1200 kms. to the west, and to carry them home to the yard. On the right-of-way near Birch Beach, in 1995, I found a five-kilo chunk of prime amethyst, the provincial stone of Ontario. (The Old Farmer's Almanac advises, "Carry amethyst for purity of heart," but I carried it no further than the floor of the car, and from there into the garden behind the house.)

Before the building of the Thunder Bay Expressway during the late 1960s, the Trans-Canada came right through the centres of Port Arthur and Fort William. While Arthur Street, the highway's route through Fort William, has been modernized almost beyond recognition, North Cumberland Street, at the Port Arthur end, is unchanged to a degree that, if you squint ever so slightly as you follow it south past the Current River, you can easily imagine yourself rolling into town in, say, a '53 four-holer, after a dusty day on the highway, looking for digs for the night. The strip is a kind of museum to a life that most parts of the city said good-bye to three or four decades ago. There are still, for instance, thirteen motels on North Cumberland, not one of them corporate-owned: the Relax, the Lakeview, the Lakehead, the

Superior, the Modern, the Sea-Vue, the Lakeshore Terrace, the Voyageur, the Old Country, the Imperial, the Swannee Cabins, the King's, and the Munro—all mod cons, and each with a view of the world's largest body of fresh water.

One of my favourites, the Modern, at number 430, displays along its fence eight or nine concrete and stone animals, life-size but of indeterminate species. My guess is that they are intended to be bears, but there are hints both porcine and bovine about them. My son Matt identified one as a rhino, because it has what appears to be a piece of deer antler protruding from the top of its snout. I once asked the owner if she knew anything about them, and she said, no, she'd only owned the motel for ten years.

When I asked how business was, she paused briefly and said, "I have nothing to complain about."

The area is serviced by businesses with names such as Gary's Auto Sales, Quick Car Repairs, Blackfoot Minnows & Live Bait, and the National Pride Car Wash.... No strip malls, no McDonald's, no Whoppers.

◆ Much has changed in Thunder Bay since those heady days when the Seaway was in its prime, the elevators were brimming, and the Keefer Terminal was unloading up to 2500 tons of goods a day.

The elevators, if it needs saying, are no long brimming, and the Keefer can go for days without seeing a ship. Our shipyard has shrivelled, our ore dock has closed and our suburbs have doubled in size. Our retail capacity has tripled and our airport quadrupled. Intercity has evolved from a verdant lowland into a consumer theme park where some of the finest trees in the city have been eliminated as an inconvenience.

During the same period of time, the city has gained an excellent spectrum of facilities for sport, entertainment, recreation and the arts. We have an attractive art gallery, a nice new museum, good libraries and a new Sports Hall of Fame. We have Magnus Theatre, the Community Auditorium, and the Thunder Bay Symphony Orchestra.... We have parks, walking paths, a college, a university and a CBC radio station...as well as funkier organizations such as the Definitely Superior art gallery and Edgy Writers in Edgy Times.

The United Grain Growers elevator on the north waterfront and the *Federal Calumet* loading at Manitoba Pool Elevator #1.

I believe that, in general, we are grateful for our cultural resources and organizations. But it is all too easy to trivialize them (as I just have) by trotting them out as totems of community prosperity, when in fact many of them are battling as frantically for their survival as is the average little business or retail store on a sidestreet in the north or south ward. During the past few years, we have seen heavy financial and staffing cuts at local CBC radio and at the Thunder Bay Public Library. We have seen an attempt to build a private condominium on the publicly owned land around Central School—a move that, had it not been brought down by indignant citizens and procedural snags, would have been fatal to the character of Waverley Park, one of the most cherished and gracious public spaces in the city. We have seen leaner operations at almost every cultural and educational institution in Thunder Bay. To be an administrator at the library, art gallery, or symphony these days—or at the museum, or Magnus, or the Sports Hall of Fame—is to be, almost by definition, a fundraiser, in addition to all the other (modestly remunerated) demands such jobs entail. An administrator at one these institutions told me recently that her salary would be laughable to someone of similar experience in industry or government; that she spends much of her time either racking her brains for money-raising ideas or actually begging for contributions; and that, at times, it all gets so pressing and discouraging that she is barely able to remember the reason for the existence of the organization she is attempting to serve and save. Some of the institutions in which we take pride would be on the slab were it not for extensive contributions from volunteers.

Despite the threat to Waverley Park and the elimination of several regional provincial parks, our city parks will survive, even thrive (the waterfront development plan is providing expansive new access to the Kam River, for example). Our college and university and libraries will pull through, too—although not necessarily in the generous forms we have known them in the past. But for our art galleries, museums, theatres, orchestras and dance troupes—and for our publishers—the battle can only get tougher. We are wealthy, yes—as long as those who nurture our treasures are willing to make the sacrifices necessary to keep doing so. Which says nothing of the survival attempts of the poets, playwrights, actors, visual artists, dancers, filmmakers and musicians, on whose efforts so many of our cultural structures are founded. I could name fifty of them, and would, except that by doing so I would slight fifty others who I could not name so readily. They are the agents of our collective imagination, and in the broadest sense are as much a part of our well-being as are the pulp mills and elevators and railways. But if they are to help sustain us as a community, we must help sustain them in return.

◆ Our artistic and recreational resources are best measured not on their own, of course, but against the greater framework of the community's health, assets and liabilities, from which they can never really be separated. At some point during Thunder Bay's 25th Anniversary celebration a couple of years ago, I was asked by Fred Jones at CBC Radio if I would come in and talk about Thunder Bay's strengths…which I was happy to do, and tried to do honestly and innocently. Needless to say, the process of identifying and selecting those strengths was highly personal and, like writing, more than a little presumptuous. I tried to choose broadly enough that the exercise wasn't just an indulgence of taste, and am happy to include my choices on these pages. With a little drum roll, then…the city's major assets, as I see them, are:

Lake Superior. I am not inclined easily to mysticism, but I know—as on some level we all know—that the lake that laps up to our doorstep is the marrow and mystery (and in some cases the money) of our days. It is also, of course, the spectacular view from so many of our lookouts and streets.

Proximity to our natural surroundings. We may be a long way from other population centres, but we're very close, both physically and psychologically, to the great non-population centres that surround us: the mountains, the forests, the Sibley Peninsula, the rocks and inland lakes. I am reminded almost daily in these parts of the degree to which land and its first cousin climate—along with our particular portion of geographical isolation—exert a constant, irreversible influence on our work, recreation, transportation, leisure, clothing, shelter, art forms, economics, history, sport, states of mind, even our dreams and mortality. "If Ireland is history," wrote Mary Frost, "northwestern Ontario is geography."

Unpretentiousness. The roots of our lack of pretensions may be various, though in the present decade most of them come down to the fact that in Thunder Bay pretensions are not part of the psychological survival code, and no one needs them to get by. The problem with this lack of airs (as I once wrote of Winnipeg) is that it sometimes takes an insidious about face, staring us down in the form of an irrational inferiority complex. When this happens, Thunder Bay need only remind itself that, by and large, it is as bright, funny, generous, understanding and daring—not to mention as timid, whiny and boring—as any town or city from New York to Vancouver to Schreiber.

I could discuss the city's assets at length—good air, sweet summers, all the facilities and parks mentioned earlier on these pages—and could think of other things to say about its liabilities. However, the more I think and talk about the place, the more I am reminded that at the core of any community, there is a knot—a complex amalgam of geography and history and fate, plus any number of unresolved hopes, frustrations and biases, interwoven

to the point that only the final shaman could ever begin to deci-
pher them.

Thunder Bay's knot is perhaps harder to untie than most right
now, because we are a city in flux and seeking direction. About
the only thing we are sure of, it seems, is that we are not about to
find that direction where others have found it in the past, and
that we must look somewhere else.

We are reminded by those in the know to remember, above all,
that we are a community not of economic indicators, but of
human beings… and that for ultimate sustainability we must look
not to Toronto, Ottawa or beyond—but within.

The notion is attractive.

Others tell us our future lies in the diligent reading of precisely those economic indicators that we have been warned to avoid.

Meanwhile, the land and lake are what they ever were, lend-
ing grace and endurance and mystery—and their own unique
measure of direction—to our sense of who we are.

Photo Credits

Front cover: courtesy of the author.

Photo: p.119, p.128; Will Carmean.

Photo: p.137; Theresa Celmer.

Photo: p.85; Pina Commisso.

Photo: p.152; Bryan Dunn.

Photo: p.89; Dominic Filane.

Photo: p.58; Lori Kiceluk.

Photos: p.44, p.46, p.52, p.54; Freda McDonald.

Photo: p.75; Shaun Naroski and Barb Kukko.

Photos: p.60, p.61, p.64; Shaun Parent.

Photos: p.2, p.26, p.29, p.122, p.123, p.135, p.145; Thunder Bay Historical Museum Society.

All other photos courtesy of the author: p.6, p.12, p.16, p.19, p.20, p.23, p.32, p.34, p.38, p.49, p.70, p.72, p.79, p.100, p,101, p.112, p.147, p.148, p.151, p.153, p.155, p.162, p.169.

Other Books by Charles Wilkins

Winnipeg 8: The Ice-cold Hothouse (ed. and co-author),
  Queenston House, 1982

The Winnipeg Book, Key Porter, 1985

Hockey: The Illustrated History, Doubleday, 1986

Paddle to the Amazon (with Don Starkell), McClelland & Stewart,
  1987

After the Applause, McClelland & Stewart, 1989

Old Mrs. Schmatterbung and Other Friends, McClelland & Stewart,
  1989

The Wolf's Eye (ed.), Thunder Books, 1992

Breakaway, McClelland & Stewart, 1995

Forever Rivals (with James Duplacey), Random House, 1996

Related Reading

The Scandinavian Home Society: A Place to Meet, A Place to Eat, Elinor Barr; the Scandinavian Home Society, Thunder Bay, 1996

Silver Islet: Striking it Rich in Lake Superior, Elinor Barr, Natural Heritage, Toronto, 1988

Branches: A Sentimental History of Fort William and Port Arthur, Bill MacDonald, Porphry Press, Thunder Bay,1990

When Trains Stopped in Dinorwic: The Story of Eric Rhind, Hazel Fulford, Singing Shield, Thunder Bay, 1990

The Survivor of the Edmund Fitzgerald, Joan Skelton, Penumbra, Moonbeam, 1985

North Country Spring, Elizabeth Kouhi, Penumbra, Moonbeam, 1993

Superior: The Haunted Shore, Wayland Drew and Bruce Litteljohn, Firefly, Toronto, 1995

Breaking the Mould: A Memoir, Penny Petrone, Guernica, Toronto, 1995

Journal of a Country Lawyer: Crime, Sin and Damn Good Fun, E.C. (Ted) Burton, Hancock House, Surrey, 1995

Killing the Shaman, James Stevens, Penumbra, Moonbeam, 1985

The Bridge Out of Town, Jake MacDonald, Oberon, Ottawa, 1986

The Wolf's Eye, Charles Wilkins (ed.), Thunder Books, Thunder Bay, 1992

Flying Colours, Rosalind Maki (ed.), Thunder Books, Thunder Bay, 1994

About the Author

Photo: Betty Carpick.

CHARLES WILKINS is the author of eight books, including the national bestseller *After the Applause* and a collection of children's verse entitled *Old Mrs. Schmatterbung and other Friends*. In 1987, he co-authored (with Don Starkell) the popular canoe adventure, *Paddle to the Amazon*. He is also a playwright and a contributor to numerous national magazines. He lives with his wife Betty Carpick and their three children in Thunder Bay, where he is at work on a book about his travels with the Great Wallenda Circus.

Index